DRESS REHEARSAL

eyelevel clubs

eight sessions for
a children's club,
plus activity day ideas

© Ro Willoughby 2009
First published 2009
ISBN 978 1 84427 383 6

Scripture Union
207–209 Queensway, Bletchley, Milton Keynes, MK2 2EB
Email: info@scriptureunion.org.uk
Website: www.scriptureunion.org.uk

Scripture Union Australia
Locked Bag 2, Central Coast Business Centre, NSW 2252
Website: www.scriptureunion.org.au

Scripture Union USA
PO Box 987, Valley Forge, PA 19482
Website: www.scriptureunion.org

Scripture quotations are from the Contemporary English Version published by HarperCollinsPublishers © 1991, 1992, 1995 American Bible Society. Anglicisations © British and Foreign Bible Society 1997.

British Library Cataloguing-in-Publication Data
A catalogue record of this book is available from the British Library.

Printed and bound in Malta by Melita Press

Cover design: kwgraphicdesign
Cover and internal illustrations: Ben Mounsey
Internal design and layout: kwgraphicdesign

ॐ Scripture Union is an international charity working with churches in more than 130 countries, providing resources to bring the good news of Jesus Christ to children, young people and families and to encourage them to develop spiritually through the Bible and prayer.

As well as our network of volunteers, staff and associates who run holidays, church-based events and school Christian groups, we produce a wide range of publications and support those who use our resources through training programmes.

Dress Rehearsal is an *eye level* club programme, part of *eye level*, Scripture Union's project to catch up with children and young people who have yet to catch sight of Jesus. For details of other *eye level* club resources and additional **Dress Rehearsal** material visit www.scriptureunion.org.uk/eyelevel

With thanks to Karen Evans, Mike Jiggins, Helen Jones, Nina Marcel and Alex Taylor of Scripture Union Publishing.

This is dedicated to all those within Scripture Union who have let me share with them in introducing children and young people to Jesus Christ.

Ro Willoughby

Contents

Starting out

Introducing Dress Rehearsal

Children love being involved in putting on a show – practising and performing on the stage, preparing costumes and props, designing promotional material, programmes and tickets and then receiving the applause! That's why the Scripture Union holiday club programme *Showstoppers!* was written – five Bible stories that must be passed on to the next generation, explored and presented to parents and carers in a grand show finale!

Dress Rehearsal follows on from *Showstoppers!* But it is a programme that can just as easily be used on its own, without any connection to the holiday club. Of course, the aim of this club, as with the holiday club, is not just to put on a show, but to introduce children to Jesus. You would not want the show preparations to eclipse the spiritual opportunities!

It would be hard in a weekly club of 60 to 90 minutes to prepare for the sort of show that might follow on from a holiday club. There isn't the time, the intensity of relationships, or the commitment of team members. On the other hand, there is the huge advantage of seeing children week after week, building normal relationships that are all part of the routine of living. 'Showtime' in *Dress Rehearsal* is the final part of each session, with parents and carers being invited to come ten minutes before the end to discover what the children have been doing in the club-time. This means that in *Dress Rehearsal* relationships are built with parents as well as children.

Must Know Stories

There are eight sessions, all of which focus around one key Bible story. Five of these stories are found in the *Must Know Stories*, which are the ten Bible stories voted as those that must be passed on to the next generation. They are written in three formats: for adults, children

aged 8 to 11 and 5 to 8. You may want to give each child a copy of the appropriate book at the end of the programme. Would church members be prepared to sponsor the purchase of a copy for each child who comes? For more details see page 61.

Into the Bible

All eight Bible stories can be found in the child-friendly book *Into the Bible – 101 Routes to Explore*. This book (with cartoon drawings and oodles of useful information) is published by Scripture Union and contains 101 key Bible passages in the Contemporary English Version. It was originally part of a primary schools' resource for RE lessons, with a CD-ROM that includes 24 lesson outlines and downloadable resources. The lessons are suitable to use as part of a local RE syllabus.

But the book itself is also ideal to use with non-church children in a Christian setting who find a whole Bible intimidating with its size, columns and small print. *Into the Bible* introduces them to Bible reading and the big Bible story in an age-appropriate way.

Dress Rehearsal DVD

Experience shows that people who lead midweek clubs like to use a variety of media and have appreciated the eye level DVDs. The *Dress Rehearsal* DVD has been put together from the wealth of Scripture Union's archive material so that for each session there is either a retold illustrated Bible story or a PowerPoint presentation to help you tell the story. Children do watch a lot of television but they may not often watch and share a programme with others, including interested adults. Even at school there will be a definite education focus to any television viewing. So this could be quite a unique experience for them.

(There is also a suggestion in each session to enable you to tell the story in another way, which includes reading it from *The 10 Must Know Stories*.)

Showtime

Each Bible story is explored using a different medium (as with *Showstoppers!*) and the last ten minutes parents/carers will be invited in for a show-and-tell. This communicates the performance element without all the hassle. The suggestions are very simple but give plenty of scope for those with extra time and imagination.

Please note: The final session is focused around the end of time with a wedding banquet. This will take some effort to set up. Do read pages 41–44 before you even begin the programme as this is the climax of *Dress Rehearsal*.

The aims of Dress Rehearsal

Children need to know that God loves them – and he loves them even when they mess up. From the moment when human beings decided to disobey God, God has been reaching out to his world, making it possible for people to come back into relationship with him. Such a relationship makes all the difference to how a child understands life, develops as a person and as a member of the community. This is the BEST good news that we can ever share!

Tragically, the majority of children know nothing about Jesus and have had little to do with his followers. But Jesus commissioned his followers to welcome children and to share his love with them and to tell them the BIG story. That's what *Dress Rehearsal*, as another programme in the *eye level* series, is all about!

For those who have run a *Showstoppers!* holiday club, *Dress Rehearsal* is a valuable tool to keep in contact with holiday club children throughout the year. For more information on how you can expand the contact you have with holiday club children throughout the year, visit the holiday club website. Even if you haven't run a holiday club, this website has great advice and stories on other ideas you can use to meet with children who have yet to catch sight of Jesus.

Boys

Recently in education circles there has been a growing concern about how many boys are being failed by the education system. This should concern those who are working in the church, not only because there are usually far more women then men in church anyway, but also because what is happening in schools is paralleled by what happens in church. Are boys being served as well as girls? Of course, it is impossible and unhelpful to speak of 'all boys being the same'.

Aims

- To welcome children into a regular club situation with lots of fun so that they can experience God's love in a community of Jesus' followers.
- To share some of the really BIG stories in the Bible.
- To use a variety of activities and learning styles that challenge children to make steps of commitment to Jesus.
- To build relationships with family members of children in the club.
- To provide opportunities for children to perform for their families.
- To follow up the *Showstoppers!* holiday club programme (as overleaf).

Many boys prefer to learn by being active. They like discovery and experimentation. Often their ability to read and use language is not as developed as it is for girls. Many boys find it hard to sit still – this is not because they are naughty but physically they find it tough. *Pretty much everything you need to know about working with 5–7s* (SU 978 184427 305 8) contains some extremely useful input on the differences between girls and boys.

- Look at the detail of your programme to see how much sitting still, reading or abstract thinking is being asked of everyone.
- You will notice that 'construction' is the word used in *Dress Rehearsal* instead of 'craft'. This is deliberate since craft can be seen as girly!
- If you include singing, is it the sort of music that boys hear around them in their world?
- Putting on a show involves lots of potentially 'male' activities with lighting, sound systems and so on. Can you accommodate those who are interested in this?
- Look at your promotional material to check how appealing it is for men, by the colours and images used.
- Male role models are vital, so strive hard to involve as many men and older boys in your activities. Remember too that boys who have grown up in the church will be more accepting of the 'way things are done'! Those who are not from a church background (who are being catered for in *Dress Rehearsal*) will be less comfortable!

The Dress Rehearsal programme

BIBLE STORY	INTO THE BIBLE REFERENCE (R = route)	DRESS	SHOWTIME
Noah	R3, R4 Genesis 6:13–18; 8:20–22	Wet weather clothes	Sound story
The Ten Commandments	R19, R20 Exodus 19:3–8, 16–20; 20:1–17	Dirty clothes	Service in community
Jeremiah the potter	R44, R45 Jeremiah 18:1–13,18; 31:31–34	Protective clothing	Clay models
Feeding over 5,000	R82 John 6:1–13	Sun hat	Cookery
The Good Samaritan	R75 Luke 10:25–37	Sling, plaster, bandage	Mime
The tale of two sons	R77 Luke 15:11–32	Old clothes and shoes	Painting/drama
Jesus' trial	R58, R59, R61 Matthew 27:15–26, 27–32; 28:1–10	Something red	Collage
The end of time	R101 Revelation 21:1–6; 22:1–5	Wedding or party clothes	Wedding finery

How to use Dress Rehearsal

The activities in *Dress Rehearsal* make very few assumptions about children's previous knowledge of the Bible or experience of a Christian community. There is plenty of scope for relationship building – with each other and God – within the orderly framework of a midweek or weekend club. Adults and children will be doing things together. Over the weeks trust will grow, as will the questions children ask and the answers they find, whether this is the first time they have been part of anything Christian or they are already part of a church community.

All activities are appropriate for any child aged 5 to 11 but be aware that you will need to adapt them if older children require a more sophisticated feature for the performance. If breaking into smaller groups for 'Look in the mirror', it would be appropriate to put the children into specific age groups.

Features of Dress Rehearsal

Clothes – dressing up
Children are invited to dress up in some way for each session. Suggestions are simple (this

should not become burdensome for parents nor be competitive). Ensure that clothes are labelled or easy to identify. No clothes should be brand new or of sentimental value. You may need to point this out in the advertisements and invitations. You will need to ensure that you have alternatives for children who arrive without the suggested clothing. You could take a photo every week of the children to keep a record of what they were wearing. You will need parental permission for this but these photos could be mounted as a display, in the same way that photos of actors in costume are on view in a theatre.

Session aim
Each session has two aims, one that outlines the Bible story and the other that states what you might expect the children to learn and how they might grow in their faith. Remember that as an *eye level* programme, *Dress Rehearsal* is specifically written with unchurched children in mind so no assumptions are made about their knowledge or experience of God or the Bible. Your task is to faithfully present God so that the Holy Spirit can give understanding and prompt a response! It is always helpful at the end of the session to review how far you achieved the original aim.

Bible

There is one Bible story per session, five of which are retold in *The 10 Must Know Stories*. Each story can obviously be found in the Bible but can also be read in *Into the Bible*. The Bible reference is given as well as the *Into the Bible* reference, which always begins with 'R' (meaning 'Route' – there are 101, not all are used in this programme). Whatever you do, make sure that you tell the story as effectively as possible and also help the children to read the Bible for themselves, or listen to it, as appropriate. Long after we have lost contact with the children, they may still have or may encounter a Bible. If we have taught them how to use it and been enthusiastic, they may go on to become lifelong Bible readers. What more could we ask?

Notes for you

Anyone engaged in children's work needs to understand a child's world, to build effective bridges into their lives. Some background information is also provided to help in your spiritual preparation.

Words from the prompter

Every dress rehearsal and performance needs a prompter to ensure things run smoothly – this is you! Practical suggestions and advice will help you run the session smoothly. Not all the suggested parts of the programme have to be included nor do they have to be in the order given. You must adapt them to suit your situation. The times given for each activity are approximate!

Note: no suggestions have been made in *Dress Rehearsal* for any songs but you can obviously choose some if the children are going to want to sing. However, do make sure that any songs are child-friendly and contain words suitable for those who may not yet know God. We should never put words into the mouths of children that they are not likely to believe or understand.

Part One: On the peg

Before getting changed for a performance, an actor has to check that their costume is ready and hanging on a peg.

Welcome

Getting off to a good, calm start is important. Make sure that each child is properly registered and wears a badge of some sort so that you don't forget names. A badge is also a good way of building the club's unique identity. Extra ideas for those first few minutes (or whenever you might have a bit of extra time) are on page 17.

Whatever you do, make sure that the group feels properly welcomed and comfortable.

The Big Cloth

This is suggested as a regular feature for the start. This is a long strip of plain cloth (something that looks quality and special). Each week the children work to turn this cloth into something beautiful, by gluing, sticking or sewing on patterns and shapes, things that are beautiful or that matter to them. It can be draped off a coat stand when the children arrive and be a decorative feature of the programme. In the final session, it will be used to think about the end of time in the context of a wedding.

It happened like this: One mother worked with a few children during a series of club sessions to create a cloth about heaven. The same group of children, boys and girls, came over every now and then to add things, some of which they had brought from home. But more importantly, they came to talk and build relationships!

Games

These are always a good way to let off steam, especially if your club is straight after school when children often have lots of pent-up energy. The suggestions given are for team games around the clothes that the children have dressed up in to come to the club. Teams should be a mixture of ages and abilities if they are to be fair. They are a means of introducing the theme of the session.

Part Two: Look in the mirror

Before going on stage, every performer checks in the mirror that they look OK, with make-up, hair and costume just right!

Looking in a mirror we see ourselves and the background around us. So as we look into the Bible, we see ourselves as God sees us and we see the background too. We also see how God wants us to become! Engaging with the Bible is the main purpose of Part Two. It provides ample opportunity to chat with children, listening to their questions and comments, sharing your own insights and experiences.

Tell the story

This explores the Bible story by retelling it. You may wish to use the *Dress Rehearsal* DVD or to tell the story in some other way. If the story is one of the *Must Know* stories it is provided on pages 50–57. Most people love hearing stories, so do your best to make this one of the highlights of the session. This leads into engaging with the Bible in some way. For more details on storytelling, read *Top Tips on Sharing Bible stories* (SU, 978 184427 328 7).

Bible and me

This is a time for reading the Bible itself, either from a child-friendly Bible translation, *Into the Bible* or a copy of the passage on paper or on screen. Suggestions are given to make this as interactive as possible, whether children can or cannot read or whether or not they like reading. It is during this time that you can inspire children by your own commitment to Bible reading. You will probably want to split into smaller groups for this. It is helpful to put children in age groups since a child's reading ability is related to their age. For more ideas of how to do this, read *Top Tips on Discovering the Bible* with children – see page 63.

Learn and remember

Learning Bible verses is a great way of understanding God's truth and storing it in your mind. There are four verses for this programme, one every two weeks. Suggestions are given to help the children learn them.

Conversation with God

This is an opportunity to talk with God together. For some children, this will be an unusual thing to do but all children have an ability to respond to God even though they may not know him personally. It is this natural ability that you are tapping into. Do not rush this conversation but do not prolong it any longer than necessary!

Construction

Not everyone's favourite activity but, when called 'construction' rather than 'craft', most boys will want to get involved. Many of the suggestions are in preparation for 'Showtime'. Constructions can be a group activity or an individual one. What is made could be taken home straightaway or could be on show for some weeks – your facilities will affect what you are able to do. This is another opportunity for conversation whatever the object being made or its effectiveness.

For additional construction ideas read *Ultimate Craft* (SU 978 184427 367 6).

Part Three: Ready for the stage

Preparing for 'Showtime'

This could be the construction time and preparing to display what has been made or it could be preparing a performance. What needs to be done will affect how much time this part needs. When preparing 'Showtime', allow children to make suggestions about what could be included. Ensure that each child has something to do. Some children may want to spend time over several weeks preparing invitations for the final session, or a programme for parents and carers. In the second session, 'Showtime' consists of a challenge to do a community project. Some children may want to explore this in subsequent sessions.

'Showtime'

This is the very end of your session, a time when parents and carers should be encouraged to come into the club to see/take part in what the children have prepared. Make sure parents and carers know what they are expected to do and where they should sit, which will probably vary with each session. Decide if you are going to let them come in whenever they arrive or queue up outside your meeting place and be allowed in when you are ready. The latter option will be less intrusive on your time with the children. You will need to stick tightly to time and try to avoid children leaving in a wound-up state. Parents will not thank you for excitable children just before bedtime and the children will be less likely to remember what they have discovered about God.

After 'Showtime' you do not need to give parents a mini-sermon. They have come to see their child perform and then take them home. Make sure everyone knows about the piece of clothing for the next session and try to say goodbye to each child personally.

Storytelling

Storytelling is key to *Dress Rehearsal*. **Each week children will find out a bit more about how to live God's way, who Jesus is and what he has done for us. However, many people feel that they are not gifted in storytelling and prefer to watch a video or read the story from a children's book of Bible stories. The aim of this page is to help you rekindle what might be a dying art form.**

Know the facts

Often we think that we know a Bible story – after all, we heard it when we were children! Don't simply rely on your memory – read the Bible text through before you look at retellings of the story.

As you read you might find it helpful to jot down the order of events, key facts, key people and content of speeches. If the story contains difficult words or unfamiliar concepts think about how these can be simplified or explained as part of the story.

Different story methods

Most children learn through seeing and doing rather than by hearing alone. Involving different learning styles as you tell a story can greatly help a child's concentration and retention of the facts.

- If you can draw well or have access to picture books you could display illustrations. (Why not use *Ultimate Visual Aids* (SU 978 184427 355 3) – a CD-ROM which contains pictures of Bible characters and scenes?)
- If the story has some repeated key words, ask the children to listen out for them and then respond with actions, or play a team game and every time a particular word is mentioned the children race round their team and back to their place.
- Story bags are increasingly popular in school and you could make one of these yourself. Customise a cloth bag with the name of your group or the name *Dress Rehearsal* and each session include different items that feature in the story.
- If there are a lot of nouns then think about playing a drawing game before you tell the story or play 'Hangman' as you go through.
- Another fun way is to read the story straight from the Bible and then re-read it again with some mistakes for the children to spot.
- Children love acting and miming – particularly if everyone can be involved in a crowd scene. Alternatively, ask leaders to act or be interviewed as if they had been with Jesus.
- If you are more creative then make some simple puppets by dressing wooden spoons or sticking faces to cardboard cones.

You will probably find that different leaders enjoy different methods, so vary the storyteller through the series to give the children different learning experiences.

Start and finish well

Even if you have wonderful pictures or exciting props and puppets you will still have to relate the story in your own words. If your group has been involved in energetic games or the children are still sticky from construction, then keeping their attention is important. Start with confidence, having planned your first sentence in advance so that it grabs their imagination and finds them eager to discover what happens. The final sentence is important too – you don't want the story simply to fade away. Perhaps this sentence could sum up your main teaching point.

Telling the story

As you tell the story, use your face and voice to convey different feelings such as being happy, sad, proud, angry, surprised or worried. Try to change your pitch and tone for characters or different situations they find themselves in.

If someone is running or excited then speak more quickly, or if they are pondering something then speak more slowly. As you reach the climax of the story or just before something exciting happens pause and then speak in a quieter voice. Move around your stage area as the story changes venue and use your body and hands to mime actions such as counting the animals onto the ark or being the father looking out for the return of his lost son.

Use your voice

Make sure you speak naturally and sound interested in the story yourself – if you have to read it then know the script well enough to add expression. And finally – there is nothing that can take the place of practice, practice and even more practice!

Storytelling ideas

Here are some different storytelling methods you could use:

- Children read out parts
- Leader reads the passage and the children listen out for specific things
- Children read parts and use props
- Children act out parts
- Leader uses pictures then children act out what happened next
- Leader reads as play, children act out parts
- Children imagine the scene with eyes shut as story is read out
- Leader takes items out of story bag

See also *Top Tips on Sharing Bible Stories*, Sue Brown, Andy Gray and Gill Marchant (SU 978 184427 328 7).

Getting to know you

Building relationships

The children you'll meet at *Dress Rehearsal* live in a fast-moving, sophisticated, technology-orientated world, dominated by screens. There is so much 'stuff' demanding their attention. Rather than trying to compete with that sort of environment, offer them what they are often missing elsewhere – real communication. Concentrate on the unique opportunity you have to build relationships; listen to them, talk with them, and give them time as you show them God's love in action. That way they will get to know you, each other and God on their *Dress Rehearsal* adventure, and have a great time too!

Listening to children

All children's work requires listening – anyone building relationships with children must learn to hear what children say.

- Give a child your full attention when they are speaking to you: look at them in an accepting way, without staring them out! Some of the deepest conversations take place whilst doing things together, often because the child does not have to maintain eye contact! This is especially true for boys. What matters then is that we show we are listening without making a big issue of it. Some children chatter much more readily if they are just telling you without it necessarily feeling like a conversation.
- Try not to give any impression that you are thinking about something else, either by looking away or nodding or making a comment in a mechanical way – children will spot this a mile off!
- Don't jump to a quick conclusion, assuming you have understood everything a child has said. You are not a child and therefore will have to work hard to grasp the context and language a child is using. Do not be judgemental!
- The more you listen, the better you will be.
- Children do mutter and may not find it easy to articulate what they want to say. Be patient and if you don't hear them the first time, ask them to repeat it more slowly. They will recognise if you are genuinely interested.
- Any questions you ask should be seeking to help a child put their thoughts into words. Questions are not just to get more information but to discover how a child feels and responds! See page 12 for more information about different types of questions.

- Don't be afraid of silence – just wait! Some children just enjoy being with an adult without having to speak.
- If a child makes some form of disclosure which would suggest abuse, listen carefully – and act immediately, in line with your church's policy. See the Scripture Union website for more information on safeguarding children.

Top tips for sharing Jesus with children

- **Build strong friendships.** Be genuinely interested in their lives, homes, interests, what happens at school. These friendships will be bridges across which Jesus can walk! Ensure that these children know that you appreciate and respect them.
- **Be informed about what is happening at school and home** – it's useful to be in the know about sports' days, class excursions or family events, and these may explain why the children are excited or tired, or both!
- **Get to know the children's families.** Understand their home lives, and help their parents (or whoever is responsible for their care) know what they are learning. Children can never be divorced from their home backgrounds. Avoid talking about Mum and Dad. It's best to refer to Mum or Dad or even, 'whoever looks after you at home'.
- **Remember birthdays**, or ask someone else to take on the responsibility of noting dates and preparing cards, perhaps for the other children to sign.
- **Do as you say!** The children need to see you model what you teach them. Your friendship with Jesus matters. How else will the children see what it means in practice to be in a relationship with him?
- **Encourage everyone to join in**, adults and children alike. Create a 'we're in this together' feel to the sessions, rather than 'them and us'. Avoid organising activities where adults stand and watch. Relax, have fun and learn with the children: 'Aim to give children the best hour of their week!' Dave Connelly, Frontline Church.
- **Mind your language!** Avoid jargon words (eg sin, grace or other churchy words) and explain what you mean by things like prayer.
- **Use illustrations from everyday life to explain concepts.** Jesus taught complex truths in simple ways, eg 'You can't see wind, but you can see the effects that it has; it's the same with the Holy Spirit'. You will need to think about this before the club begins.
- **Grow the children's confidence with the Bible** and explain how to read it. Why don't we often start at page 1? How do we use the

Contents page? (Younger children find this very hard.) What are the differences between chapters and verses, or the Old and New Testaments? How do you explain that the Bible is one big story – God's story – in different bits? Find out more about the Bible in *The Story of the Book* (SU 978 184427131 3).

- **Talk about Jesus**, rather than God, where possible. The Gospels give us clear pictures of what he is like and these are far easier to grasp than the idea of God being 'up there' but invisible. Children have some very woolly ideas about God, but there is less room for manoeuvre when it comes to Jesus! You will have plenty of opportunities to talk about Jesus throughout the programme.

- **Apply the Bible teaching appropriately**: 'If Jesus arrived in your town, like he arrived in Jerusalem, what do you think he would say and do? How do you think people would welcome him?' Help them see that Jesus is alive today (even though we can't see him) and is relevant to their lives.

- **Allow children to make responses that are appropriate for them**, their understanding and their backgrounds. Don't rush straight in with, 'Do you want to follow Jesus?' That should be a decision that lasts for life, and they need to recognise what it entails. For many children, there are a number of commitments as their understanding grows.

- **Have fun together!** The children need to catch something of the 'life in all its fullness' that Jesus spoke about.

Practical considerations

Safeguarding children

It is important to think about safeguarding children when running your club. If your midweek club has already been in existence for some time, you have probably made all the necessary arrangements. However, if you are just starting up a midweek club, there is advice on child protection, registering your club, registering your children and health and safety on the Scripture Union website at www.scriptureunion.org.uk/Clubs/downloads

Working with small groups

Practicalities

- Children are all different. Respect their differences.
- Make sure any child with a special need is catered for.
- Make sure children know they can come to you with any questions.
- Make sure that children are comfortable. Cold, hard floors do not encourage positive discussion. Cushions, mats or comfortable chairs can make all the difference. Sometimes, everyone lying on their tummies in a star shape can create a fantastic atmosphere – their teacher at school is unlikely to do this!
- Keep good eye contact with every child.
- In the group, watch out for children who are on the edge.
- Don't talk down to children – talk with them. This means getting to their level, physically and verbally.
- Don't always rush to fill silences while children are thinking of responses.
- Validate all responses, either by a further question or ask others what they think, especially if you don't agree with the initial comment or answer.
- If lots of children want to talk, pass an object round – only the child holding the object can speak.
- Encourage children to listen to each other (something they might find quite difficult).
- Be prepared to admit that you don't know the answer to a question, but say that you'll find out the answer, if appropriate.

Asking questions

There are plenty of opportunities in *Dress Rehearsal* for asking the children questions about the Bible passage and encouraging their thinking about God. A discussion is most appropriate when the children are in small groups as they don't need to wait as long for an opportunity to speak.

Ever thought about the kinds of questions you ask people? The same question can be asked in many different ways, and force the person being asked the question to give certain kinds of answers.

Rhetorical

If you ask, 'Isn't it great to have ice cream?' it is a rhetorical question, implying the expected answer. It brings out the right answer for the benefit of others.

Closed

If you ask, 'Do you like coming to *Dress Rehearsal*?' it is a closed question, mainly allowing for 'Yes' or 'No'. It encourages contributions and assesses what the children think.

Factual

If you ask, 'What food did Jesus give the crowd of people?' it is a factual question, requiring basic information. It encourages contributions and establishes the facts.

Open

If you ask, 'Why did Jesus' disciples argue about who was the greatest?' it is an open question, allowing broad expression. It encourages discussion and indicates what the children think.

Experience

If you ask, 'Have you ever been in a situation where you have found it hard to give – like the rich young ruler?' it is an experience question, for sharing views or feelings. It encourages discussion and helps children to apply the teaching personally.

Leading

If you ask, 'What have you learnt at *Dress Rehearsal*, Anna?' it is a leading question aimed at getting a specific answer from someone. It indicates learning and understanding and encourages contributions.

Think about when you might use these types of questions in your group. Go through each question with your team and decide when it is appropriate and when it is inappropriate to use certain kinds of questions.

To find out more, read *Top Tips on leading small groups for children and young people* by Simon Barker and Steve Whyatt (SU 978 184427 388 1) – available October 2009.

Helping children respond

Being Jesus' friend

At *Dress Rehearsal*, the children will find out about the awesome God who loves and cares for us, and who came to rescue us and help us to be his friends. They will see that we should always thank him, and obey him. They will also learn that Jesus can forgive us for all the wrong we ever do. This may prompt the children to want to know Jesus personally. Be ready to help them.

- They rarely need long explanations, just simple answers to questions.
- Talk to them in a place where you can be seen by others.
- Never put pressure on children to respond in a particular way, just help them take one step closer to Jesus when they are ready. We don't want them to respond just to please us!
- Remember, many children make a commitment to Jesus, followed by further commitments as they mature and their understanding grows.
- Many children just need a bit of help to say what they want to say to God. Here is a suggested prayer they could use to make a commitment to Jesus:

Jesus, I want to be your friend.
Thank you that you love me.
Thank you for living in the world and dying on
*   a cross for me.*
I'm sorry for all the wrong things I have done.
Please forgive me and let me be your friend.
Please let the Holy Spirit help me be like you.

Amen.

Reassure them that God hears us when we talk with him and has promised to forgive us and help us be his friends.

To find out more, read *Top Tips on responding to Jesus* by Helen Franklin, Steve Hutchinson and Robert Willoughby (SU 978 184427 387 4) – available October 2009.

What next?

Children need help to stick with Jesus, especially if their parents don't believe.

- Assure them that God wants them to talk with him, whatever they want to say. Give them some prayer ideas.
- Encourage them to keep coming to Christian activities, not necessarily on Sundays – their 'church' might be the midweek club or a school lunchtime club.

- Reading the Bible will be easier with something like *Snapshots* – but you need to support them if they are to keep it up. It may be appropriate to give them a Bible as well. Alternatively, you may want to give them their own copy of *Into the Bible*. Make sure that this is not seen as a reward for becoming a Christian.
- Keep praying and maintain your relationship with them wherever possible.

Some booklets from Scripture Union that may help

Friends with Jesus

A booklet explaining what it means to make a commitment to follow Jesus for 8s and under.

978 1 84427 141 2 (single) £0.99
978 1 84427 144 3 (pack of 20) £15.00

Me+Jesus

A booklet explaining what it means to make a commitment to follow Jesus for 8 to 10s.

978 1 84427 142 9 (single) £0.99
978 1 84427 145 0 (pack of 20) £15.00

Jesus=friendship forever

A booklet explaining what it means to make a commitment to follow Jesus for 10 to 12s.

978 1 84427 143 6 (single) £0.99
978 1 84427 146 7 (pack of 20) £15.00

Snapshots

Bible reading for 8 to 11s
£3.00 single copy
UK £11.00 annual subscription
£15.00 packs of 6

Prices are correct at the time of going to press.

Sharing your faith

So many people put their trust in Jesus because they have heard how important he is to someone else. You have a great opportunity to share with the children what Jesus means to different people, and also to show by the way you live your own life that Jesus really is alive! Here are some pointers to bear in mind when you're talking with children about what Jesus means to you:

- Make sure you don't use Christian jargon or concepts that just don't make sense: 'Inviting Jesus into your heart' might suggest to some children that Jesus is only welcome in a bit of them. The idea of a person you can't see living inside your body can be a bit spooky!
- Remember you are talking to children whose experience of life is not as broad as an adult's, so their uncertainties and questions are different. Address their issues by referring to experiences which are relevant to them. This is not necessarily just what it was like for you when you were a child! But, for example, the emotions you experienced when you recently changed job may be very similar to those of a child changing school. God was with you then, so he can be with a child.
- Speak about Jesus as someone you know and are enthusiastic about.
- Make reference to what the Bible says in a way that makes a child want to read the Bible for themselves – sound enthusiastic about what God has said to us. Hold the Bible with respect and read it with interest. Tell a Bible story briefly to explain a point.
- Be brief and speak with simple sentences, using appropriate language.
- Be honest, talking about the good and the bad times. God doesn't always give answers straightaway, or the answers we want.
- It is important to talk about what Jesus means to us now and not when we first came to know him dozens of years ago.

If you are involved in up-front presentation, there are some other points to consider:
- An interview process is less intense and invites the children to engage with what the interviewee is saying.
- Include questions or information about subjects such as favourite colours, food, team, job, hopes, worst moments, as well as a favourite Bible character or story. Think what a child is curious about. 'Normal' information communicates that being a Christian is all about Jesus being with us all the time, being normal!
- Not everyone's experience will be appropriate, however dramatic it might be! Long and complicated stories will lose children. A wide age range of children will also determine what is suitable.
- Use someone's story that is relevant to the theme of the day.
- Over the weeks, choose a variety of people with different experiences to share what Jesus means to them.
- It would be worth the team hearing what is going to be said in advance, if someone's experience is going to raise questions that may be a challenge to answer.
- Whether you're speaking in front of the whole club, or one child, you should be ready to tell your story. Think beforehand about what you are going to say, just as you would practise music or drama. It isn't a speech but there is no excuse for rambling.

For more details on nurturing faith read *Top Tips on Encouraging faith to grow* by Piers Lane (SU 978 184427 321 8).

What to do after Dress Rehearsal

Step one – time to think

Hopefully *Dress Rehearsal* has made you think about how you run activities and reach out to children in your community. Before the end of the *Dress Rehearsal* programme, plan a review with anyone who helped. Be as honest as you can and dream dreams!

- What did the children enjoy about *Dress Rehearsal*?
- What was different compared to your previous activities for children?
- Were there more small-group activities? How did they work?
- Was there more Bible input than before?
- What worked really well or didn't work?
- What did the leaders enjoy?
- What did you discover about each other's gifts for working with children? Was there an unknown storyteller or someone especially good at welcoming children?

Write down the most important answers. Talk about what you should do next, considering the following:

- the children and their families who come – what is best for them
- other groups of people whom you might wish to contact
- the leaders who are available, or those who could be trained or invited to get involved
- the time commitment and use of premises
- the time of year and other events in the local calendar (both community and church events)
- what approaches you have seen, heard or read about that have been effective elsewhere

Step two – moving on

Don't be afraid to develop what you provide for children. If *Dress Rehearsal* encouraged you to run a midweek or Saturday club for the first time and it worked, plan to carry on. You may need extra help, especially if some people can't commit themselves weekly. Perhaps you could continue your club next term or maybe a monthly Saturday/Sunday special, using another Scripture Union programme.

Discuss how you might contact new children. What are your links with the local school(s) or neighbourhood groups? For more ideas on building bridges between local schools and the community see *Top Tips on Developing partnerships between church and school* (SU 978 1 84427 339 3). Could you publicise your group through the local paper or library? How could

the children who already come be encouraged to bring their friends? Just how many more children can you cope with?

Step three – building on Dress Rehearsal

One of the aims of *Dress Rehearsal* is to bring children who don't usually have much contact with a Christian community into a Christian activity. If this worked for you, build on the final *Dress Rehearsal* session and get to know the children's families by running a parents' special event. Family games work well, either games to play within families or families competing against one another. Any family activity that offers food will be popular! Alternatively, some churches have explored parenting groups. In one place a church football team has developed from fathers of children who started coming to a church children's club. Be imaginative and find out what other churches have done in your area. Maybe you could do something together.

Whatever you do, try to maintain contact with children, to sustain and grow your relationships. You may wish to visit them at home, to deliver a birthday card or to let parents know the starting date for next term, or to invite families to a family event or special service such as a carol service. If you do home visits make sure parents are happy for you to come and contact them to arrange a time for your visit.

Other programmes

If you have done *Dress Rehearsal* as part of a longer-term club (either to start the club off, or as a continuation of an existing club), look out for these other resources from SU which are similar in aim and design to *Dress Rehearsal*:

Target Challenge, High Five!, So Why God?, Rocky Road, Clues2Use, Awesome!, and *Streetwise*.

If you want to put on a holiday club, look out for the following resources from SU:

*Showstoppers!, Champion's Challenge, Wastewatchers, Pyramid Rock, Landlubber*s and *Xpedition Force.*

These resources are available from good local Christian bookshops or from SU Mail Order:
Scripture Union Mail Order,
PO Box 5148,
Milton Keynes MLO,
MK2 2YX.
Tel: 0845 07 06 006
Fax: 01908 856020
Web: www.scriptureunion.org.uk

Other ministries

X:site

X:site is a children's event for 7- to 11-year-olds. Each event takes place every two months in towns, cities or whole areas and combines silly games, live music, videos, creative prayer, craft, drama, Bible stories and lots more so that everyone can learn about Jesus and have fun at the same time!

X:site is a great way to encourage children in your church by bringing them together with other children in their community – they will have such a good time that they will want to invite their friends to come too. X:site is organised in each area by a partnership of local churches; Scripture Union is really keen to see more X:site events happening around the country. With your help there could be one nearer you. Check out the X:site website (www.xsiteuk.org) and if you want to get involved get in touch with us. We would really love to hear from you!

Families' ministry

Of course, children belong to their wider family and in running *Dress Rehearsal* you will meet different family members especially because of the showtime at the end of each session! Any child's commitment to follow Jesus will have an impact upon their family. *Dress Rehearsal* gives you opportunities to extend the church's families' ministry, both to those within the church and those who do not have many links with church.

Some parents like to help at church children's activities, even if they would not describe themselves as Christians. Parents are often open to meet with other parents to discuss the joys and challenges of parenting, whether this is for new parents, or parents of teenagers. What parenting support can you offer? For more details of the resources Scripture Union offers visit www.scriptureunion.org.uk/families.

There is also an online six-session course based on the book *Families with faith: Survival skills for Christian parents* by Richard Patterson (SU 978 184427 247 1), which is available on the website. The course is called *Survival skills for Christian parents*. This is also suitable for parents who are not Christians but want to look at life from a Christian perspective. For details of family ministry opportunities read *Top Tips on Growing faith with families* (SU 978 184427 249 5) and for consideration the implications of working with children from other faith backgrounds, read *Top Tips on Welcoming children of other faiths* (SU 978 184427 250 1).

Specific Dress Rehearsal opportunities

Building on the costume theme of *Dress Rehearsal* you could arrange a family evening or morning. These are aimed at being cross-generational and appealing to those who are in the church and those who are not yet there! For example:

Mums and daughters: lots of fun can be had for all ages of women and girls with make-up, hair-braiding, manicures (or even pedicures), face painting, head massage, a one-off fitness programme. Charity shops have been known to lend their clothes to a church group who have then arranged a fashion parade. This does not have to be of the standard of a Paris catwalk, and no one would expect that, but can be great fun. It all depends upon who you know to offer their advice and expertise.

Dads and sons: dressing up to go on a night hike is an adventure (and girls would enjoy this too but boys may prefer it if it is a 'men only event'!) Boys with absent fathers could be included, so long as you follow the Child Protection Policy of the church. The hike does not have to be all-night and is not complicated to organise.

School uniform parade: just before the start of the new academic year you could arrange a special event for those who are beginning at a new school. Children could come in their new uniform with a parent or carer. The programme could include a snack, a discussion about fresh starts (parents and children could be separated for this) and conclude with a prayer of blessing for parents and children. Non-Christians expect Christians to pray so it is wholly appropriate for the church to pray for families at such a time of transition. The timing of this event is crucial. Local schools could send out invitations before the end of the school year (although people may forget over the holidays). Think how else you might advertise, what personal contacts there are, where you could put posters and where you might hold the event. If held in a local school it would have a natural appeal.

Extra activities

The first and last few minutes of a club can be the most important! Your first conversation with a child helps to settle them, for them to be open to God. You represent Jesus: your welcome is his welcome. The end of the club may be what they remember best, so make the most of the time.

A few guidelines

- Choose the right opening question for the right day: if it's the weekend, keep school conversation to a minimum.
- Be led by the child. Don't probe where they don't want to talk.
- Allow a conversation to develop rather than just asking questions.
- Help others join in as they join the group.
- Tell the children about your day to build friendships and make it less like a grilling.

Questions about school

What was the best thing that happened? Did anything funny happen? What did you have for dinner? What's the food like at your school?

General questions

What have you seen on television/read/done recently? What are you doing this weekend?

How's your football team doing? Tell me about your family/pets/what you do in your spare time.

Ideas to end the club

A routine pattern to the end may be useful:

In groups

- Chat about what they will do at home/later/during the week.
- A quick recap of the Bible teaching to help them remember/apply it.
- Pray for the week ahead.

Together

- Recap the Bible teaching and allow a moment to think about it again.
- Sing the same song each week, making it a theme song for the club.

One after-school club always concludes with a short prayer followed by a 'wind-up Amen' where everyone starts saying, 'Amen' softly and ends up shouting it. One classroom teacher asked a leader of the club what it was that the children always shouted at the end! It was a good opening to share about prayer!

Other extra activities

- **Turn everyone's name round** and enjoy the different sounds! (Nhoj Htims, Enna Senoj)
- **I Spy**. For very young children, play 'I spy with my colour eye', with objects of a certain colour.
- **Who can…** wiggle their ears, touch their nose with their tongue, recite the alphabet backwards, wiggle their eyebrows and so on.
- **Dice games**: have ready-made cards with questions to be answered when the numbers are rolled. For example:
  Favourites:
    1 – food
    2 – pop group
    3 – team
    4 – TV programme
    5 – story
    6 – colour
  Home:
    1 – family
    2 – rooms
    3 – pets
    4 – food
    5 – outside the house
    6 – favourite room
  Favourite food:
    1 – sandwich
    2 – drink
    3 – breakfast
    4 – biscuits
    5 – snack
    6 – worst food
- **'I went to the park** (supermarket, football match) and I saw…' Each person recites the growing list and adds an item.
- **Mime** things you do at home – others must guess, eg watching TV, turning on a tap, cleaning teeth.
- Challenge the group to use their bodies to **make a human sculpture** of household objects, eg a chair, knife and fork, clock, bathroom.

Session 1

Noah and the flood
Genesis 6; 8:20–22; 9:8–13,17
(**Into the Bible** R3, R4)

Aims

To explore what had gone wrong with the world and what God promised

To recognise that God can wipe the board clean when we do wrong and he keeps his promise

Clothes
Wet weather clothes

Notes for you

A child's world: Every single child in the session, just like every adult too, has a natural tendency to do wrong. But often people like to think someone else is to blame. Some children will have a clear sense of what it means to do the right or wrong thing as far as God is concerned; others will always think someone else is to blame and certainly not them; others because they have such a poor image of themselves will automatically think they have done wrong and would find it impossible to accept that God might think they had any value at all. So think carefully about how you will talk about sin and wrong-doing. Focus upon God's desire to relate to Noah and his promise to him.

God's promise to Noah

Part one
On the peg

01 Welcome

Greet each child personally, reminding parents and carers that they are welcome to come ten minutes before the end of the session to see the session's 'Showtime'. Draw attention to the coat stand or the hanger where the Big Cloth is hanging - see page 7.

You could take photos of the children arriving in their wet weather clothes which could be shown in a compilation of images of *Dress Rehearsal* in the final 'Showtime'. Make sure that you have parents' permission to do this. As this is the first session of the club, some children may not have remembered to bring wet weather clothes with them, so have some on hand for those who have not come suitably dressed.

Provide some badge-making resources (stickers, felt-tip pens etc) and help each child make a name badge.

If you have decided to create the Big Cloth (see page 7), you will need to explain that in the final session you will be using this piece of cloth, but at the moment it looks rather boring. Over the next few weeks, the children will make it beautiful by sticking or sewing or painting or spraying on beautiful objects. Help the children to begin work on this. For this first session, provide a selection of items they can use to decorate the cloth, for example, material that looks like water or some animal shapes. For future sessions, encourage the group to bring in pieces of shiny cloth, furry material or anything that looks, feels or smells special.

02 Games
10 minutes

You will need
• props for your chosen games

Play a series of relay races with teams that are mixed age and ability. Try out some of these variations, making sure you risk assess the option you have chosen:
• Children race in the wet-weather clothes that they have brought with them.
• Give each team a pair of adult boots. The first person in the team puts the boots on and walks to the end of the room and back. They then take the boots off and give them to the next person.
• Give each team a pile of beanbags. In turn, each member of the team has to run to the other side of the room and throw a beanbag into one of four or five upturned umbrellas (each with a different points' value).

Games that use water would be suitable for the theme but they can make everyone and everything rather wet. If you have the space and the facilities to help everyone dry off, then these kinds of games will be a memorable experience for the children!

Part two
Look in the mirror

01 Tell the story
5 minutes

You will need

• The *10 Must Know Stories* or the story 'Boat building on dry land' from page 50, and/or the *Dress Rehearsal* DVD

Either read the story 'Boat building on dry land' from page 8 of *The 10 Must Know Stories* or from page 50. Alternatively, (or in addition)

18

1

show episode 1 of the *Dress Rehearsal* DVD.

If you're reading the story, omit the sound instructions on your first reading. Try to create a warm atmosphere as the storyteller shares this special story with the children. Make sure everyone is 'sitting comfortably so you can begin'! Practise reading it so that you can read with expression and enthusiasm. (See page 9 for tips on storytelling.)

2 2 Bible and me
10 minutes

You will need
- copies of Genesis 9:8–13,17 (Bibles, *Into the Bible* R4 or paper copies)
- A3 sheets of paper and felt-tip pens (including all the rainbow colours)

Once the children know the story, turn to Genesis 9:8–13,17, (the second part of R4 in *Into the Bible*). Make sure everyone can see the Bible text.

Explain that Noah has come out of the big boat along with his family and all the animals and birds. God speaks to him again. Ask a confident reader to read these verses or do so yourself.

Give everyone a piece of paper and a felt-tip pen and ask the following questions. (This should not be too much like school.)
- God makes a solemn promise to three groups. **Who are they?** In pairs, ask the children to quickly sketch just one of these groups. After two minutes, see how many children drew Noah, animals and birds, or people who lived after Noah. Comment appreciatively on the drawings and did anyone draw themselves? They could have done.
- What did God promise?
- What sign did God give that he would keep his promise?

On another large piece of paper see if together you can draw a large rainbow getting the colours in the right order. (You'll be using this rainbow in Conversation with God.)

Give one personal example where God has kept his promise to you. It needs to be an experience children can relate to, such as God being with you at a time when you were scared or sad.

2 3 Learn and remember
5 minutes

You will need
- whiteboard with pen
- cleaning cloth

Remind the children that the flood happened because God was angry with how people were behaving. They did not listen to him. Their relationship with him was broken. The Bible calls this 'sin'. But God forgives anyone who asks him. Once he has forgiven us it is just as if we have done nothing wrong. Scribble on the board so that it looks really messy (you could ask a child to help scribble). Explain that another way of looking at it is as though God sees scribbly writing on a whiteboard and he wipes it clean. As you say this, wipe the board clean.

A man called King David, who was king of God's people a long time after Noah lived, had broken God's rules about marriage and murder. He did not realise he had done wrong until someone pointed it out to him. Then he put these words into a song in a book called Psalms (it's chapter 51). He knew he could ask God to forgive him. If you are using *Into the Bible* look up R36.

> 🎵 *You are kind, God!*
> *Please have pity on me …*
> *Please wipe away my sins.* 🎵
> Psalm 51:1

Write these words on the whiteboard. Say them twice, then gradually remove a few words at a time until there is nothing left. The whiteboard is wiped clean but the words are printed on the children's memories! Check that the children have remembered this at the end of 'Showtime'! It will be a chance to tell parents about what else is included in the programme.

2 4 Conversation with God
5 minutes

You will need
- the drawing of the rainbow
- Post-it notes
- pens

Give each child a Post-it note and ask them to write or draw something they want to thank God for. Suggest that they could thank God that he wipes the board clean, if we ask him to take away the wrong things we do, think or say. But many children will have no sense that sin has broken their relationship with God so don't labour this point! Invite the children to stick their Post-it note around the drawing of the rainbow, remembering that God keeps his promise.

Words from the prompter

The creative medium to be explored in this session is that of making a sound picture. You can share the story of Noah with the audience of parents and carers at the end of the session, using an imaginative range of relevant background sounds. Suggestions are made for how to do this but your imagination and that of the children should mean that the final 'performance' is much fuller than is given below in 'Preparing for Showtime'. Where possible, encourage the children to wear their wet weather clothes for 'Showtime' to reinforce that this is a real dress rehearsal.

1

❷❺ Construction
10 minutes

You will need
- a large potato for each child
- coloured drawing pins
- felt-tip pens
- thick plastic cut into circles (10 cm diameter)
- scissors
- cocktail umbrellas
- stapler
- wool or straw

Make a potato head, by sticking pins for eyes and drawing on nostrils and mouth. Wool or straw hair could be added. Cut a quarter out of the circle of plastic and staple together what's left to make a rain hat. Attach this on the top of the potato man using the cocktail umbrella. During construction time talk with (and listen to) the children to get to know them. But as appropriate, ask them what they thought was the best bit about the story of Noah.

A larger group version of the 'potato head' could be made using a round pumpkin or squash, cutting out eyes, a nose and mouth, sticking on an enlarged hat and creating an umbrella with a bendy straw, covered with thin card. Older children might like to think how to make an umbrella, using kebab sticks and isosceles triangles of material or card.

These could all be displayed at the end.

Part three
Ready to go on stage

❸❶ Preparing for Showtime
15 minutes

Use the story 'Boat building on dry land' from *The 10 Must Know Stories* or from page 50. Divide the children into three groups (though if the club is small, all the children can do everything). With two practices the groups should come in at the right time, and if they don't, this is only the dress rehearsal! But you could make a list of the order of sounds so that children will know when it is their group's turn. One leader should act as the 'conductor', so emphasise that everyone should keep an eye on this conductor to know when to come in and when to stop. The 'orchestra' will be on view so you could decide on some simple actions, such as everyone looking startled when the door bangs shut.

One person should read out the words God says – they will need a script. A leader (or very competent child) can play the narrator.

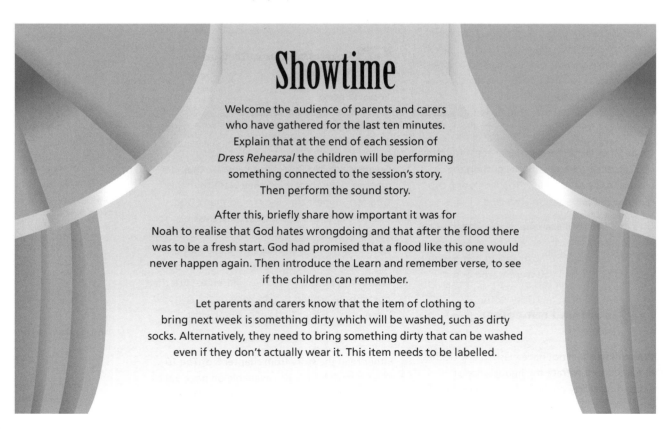

Showtime

Welcome the audience of parents and carers who have gathered for the last ten minutes. Explain that at the end of each session of *Dress Rehearsal* the children will be performing something connected to the session's story. Then perform the sound story.

After this, briefly share how important it was for Noah to realise that God hates wrongdoing and that after the flood there was to be a fresh start. God had promised that a flood like this one would never happen again. Then introduce the Learn and remember verse, to see if the children can remember.

Let parents and carers know that the item of clothing to bring next week is something dirty which will be washed, such as dirty socks. Alternatively, they need to bring something dirty that can be washed even if they don't actually wear it. This item needs to be labelled.

The Ten Commandments

Part one
On the peg

01 Welcome

Greet each child personally, reminding parents and carers that they are welcome to come ten minutes early to see this week's 'Showtime'. Draw attention to the coat stand or the hanger where the Big Cloth is hanging.

You could take photos of the children arriving in their dirty clothes which could be shown in a compilation of images of *Dress Rehearsal* in the final 'Showtime'. Make sure that you have parents' permission to do this.

Make sure any new child has been given or made a badge.

If you have decided to make the Big Cloth (see page 7), explain what this is to any new children or to those who have forgotten. Any child who has brought something to stick on the cloth should do so early on in the session as other children arrive.

02 Games
10 minutes

You will need

- Bowls with warm water
- scrubbing brushes
- rubber gloves
- washing powder/liquid suitable for hand washing
- spin dryer (optional)
- clothes line and pegs
- dirty tea towels or bits of cloth for those who have not brought any dirty clothes
- plastic bags to take home damp clothes/ material

Most children will not have washed any clothes by hand. Demonstrate the importance of rubbing two dirty pieces of fabric against each other, dipping it regularly into the water. Ensure that rubber gloves are worn and warn the children not to rub so hard that they get blisters. Resistant dirt could be helped with a scrubbing brush or washing liquids that claim to remove resistant stains. Once the clothes are fairly clean, wring them out, and peg them on a washing line. Use a spin dryer if at all possible.

Alternatives: You could show children how to clean shoes with polish. This will require leather shoes, polish or cream, brushes and cloths. It will be a novel experience for many children!

You could also show children how to remove specific stains on washable fabrics. For example: iron or rust stains respond to lemon juice and salt; paint or felt-tip stains using white spirit; curry stains, soaked in lukewarm water then rubbed with equal parts of glycerine and water and rinsed in water; wax candle, using a warm iron on paper towel underneath and on top of the affected area; blood stains, soaked in several changes of very cold salty water, then use biological detergent; beetroot stains, soaked in cold water rubbing washing-up liquid in the affected area. Try all these out beforehand and supervise well if using anything potentially dangerous, such as an iron or white spirit.

Part two
Look in the mirror

21 Tell the story
5 minutes

You will need

- The *10 Must Know Stories* or the story as printed on page 52, and/or the *Dress Rehearsal* DVD

Either read the story from chapter 3 of *The 10 Must Know Stories* (also available on page 52) or show episode 2 of the *Dress Rehearsal* DVD. Try to create a warm atmosphere as the storyteller

Session 2

God gives Moses the Ten Commandments
Exodus 19:3–8,16–20; 20:1–17
(**Into the Bible** R19, R20)

Aims
To hear how, because God loved his people so much, he gave them rules so that they could live the best way possible

To explore what it means for us to do what pleases God

Clothes
Dirty ones, to wear and to wash (which may or may not be the same)

Notes for you
A child's world: Children are very familiar with rules and laws. In school there will be rules that have been agreed in the classroom, such as listening to each other. There will also be rules for the whole school, such as no running down the corridor or closing the gate once the school day has started. Rules are really in everyone's best interests but in society the law tends to be seen as something irksome, or to be complained about when others break the law. It is important that children see that the law is evidence of God's goodness and love for his people. What is more, he helps us to do what is right, to keep his rules.

2

Words from the prompter

The 'creative medium' used in this session is that of doing something to help the community. In 'Showtime', there will not be a performance but parents and carers will hear what the children are going to do over the next few weeks to help others. You hope that their creativity has been stimulated and channelled! You will need to have done preparation before the session to work out what sort of project would be feasible. Factors to consider are:

- The size of your group
- The amount of time available – can things be done outside club time?
- The skill of leaders
- The support of parents and carers
- The age of children and how responsible they are
- The time of year – summer is a better time for outdoor and nature activities
- The needs of the community

Suggested community projects:

- Bake some cakes and either give them to cheer up others or sell them to raise money for a chosen suitable charity. These could be attractively packaged in boxes or bags that the children have decorated.
- Make bird boxes or bird feeders as a contribution to the environment.
- Organise a carwash – this needs careful supervision but can be great fun and very wet.
- Make windmills for gardeners to put

shares this story with the children. Make sure everyone is 'sitting comfortably so you can begin'! Practise reading it so that you can read with expression and enthusiasm. The comments on each of the Ten Commandments could be read by another reader. Ask the children to listen out for why people had to have clean clothes.

2 2 Bible and me
10 minutes

You will need
- copies of Exodus 19:3–8, Bibles or copies of *Into the Bible*, picture of an eagle (see page 59)

Once children know the story, turn to Exodus 19:3–8 or use R19 from *Into the Bible*. Make sure each child can see either a Bible or a photocopy of this part of the Bible story.

Explain that God's people had been slaves in Egypt but God had rescued them. He had done this because he loved them. He went on to protect them and provide them with food and drink as they wandered around in the desert – all this because he loved them. But he also wanted them to know the best way to live their lives, in the same way that an adult bird looks after its young.

Show the picture of the eagle and talk together about how young birds are nurtured and prepared for life.

Read together Exodus 19:3–8, asking the children to look at how many times the word 'You' occurs. Ask the children to comment on what each 'you' is about:

You – saw the exodus/rescue from Egypt.

You – knew how God had brought the people to this point

You – are to faithfully obey God

You – will be God's holy nation/special people

You – will do everything the Lord has commanded

Point out that the people had to make themselves ready and clean to meet God. They had to obey God's commands (and ask how many of the Ten Commandments the children can remember). But in return, they were going to be God's special people and they were going to know God's care and protection. In the Bible, the two always go together – knowing we are special to God and obeying him!

2 3 Learn and remember
5 minutes

You will need
- each word of this verse written on a different piece of paper or cloth

Last session's Learn and remember verse is appropriate for this session too. See how many children can remember it. Hide the pieces of paper or cloth around the room. Once the children have found them, challenge them to put the verse together.

> Ⓖ *You are kind, God! Please have pity on me... Please wipe away my sins.* Ⓖ
> *Psalm 51:1*

Comment that this is all about God doing things to show his love for us. On this occasion there is nothing about us having to do anything to experience God's kindness.

2 4 Conversation with God
5 minutes

You will need
- picture of an eagle (see page 59)

Sit round in a circle and remind the children of how God is like an eagle, caring for its young. Talk about how God cares for us. Give the children several sentences of thanks, thanking God that he cares for us, gives us food and drink, clothes to keep us warm, and keeps us safe. Then pass the picture around the group. As each child holds it, they speak out one sentence thanking God for how he loves us or cares for us. It does not matter if children say the same thing. Assume that each child will want to join in but if a child hesitates, assure them it is OK to pass the picture on to the next child. If you are a large group, split into smaller ones.

2 5 Construction
10 minutes

You will need
- pieces of white rag (about 10 cm square)
- art materials (paint and brushes, felt-tip pens etc)
- stencils (optional)

Give out the pieces of rag to the children and ask them to decorate them with a design of their choice. They could draw a scene from the story, illustrate one of the Ten Commandments or simply do their own design. You could provide stencils to help the children make an interesting pattern – stencils of numbers would be good. These rags could be taken home or sewn/stuck onto the Big Cloth. You could also turn the rag into a flag or frame it.

Part three
Ready to go on stage

🕒1 Preparing for 'Showtime'
15 minutes

Explain that God gave his rules or commandments to the people because he wanted them to live together happily as a community, caring for one another. Talk about how important it is that we care for one another in our families, at school and around where we live.

Tell the group that over the next few weeks, you're going to be doing a community project together. Give the children a maximum of three possibilities of what you might do. Write them up on a board and explain what they are. Discuss with the children the advantages and disadvantages, letting them make their contribution. Record what is said on the board. It is really important that children feel that this is their project. Finally decide on what you are going to do and how. Remember – don't commit yourselves to doing something you cannot complete!

Complete the project plan as laid out on the right: Be as specific as you can.

in their gardens as decoration or even to act as scarecrows.
- Paint or decorate a flower pot or arrange some dried flowers for an elderly person.
- Plant bulbs, lettuce seeds or vegetables and watch them grow over the next few weeks. These can be given to others.
- Make Christmas cards and sell them for an appropriate charity.
- Collect children's clothes to send to a charity working with children in need. This builds on the overall theme of the **Dress Rehearsal**.
- Set the children a task that they can do in their home. This will need parental collaboration. You could make a card that parents tick off over the length of **Dress Rehearsal** to keep a check on how far the children have managed to help in their homes.

Showtime

Welcome the audience of parents and carers and explain that at the end of each session of *Dress Rehearsal* they will be experiencing something connected to the session's story. Tell the audience about the community project, making it clear what parents and carers are, or are not, being asked to do. Ask for volunteers as required.

After this, briefly share how God gave his people rules so that they could live together happily in a community, which is why you are doing this project. God gave them these rules because he loved them. You could conclude by asking the children how many of the Ten Commandments they can remember. If the children painted any of the commandments onto their white rags, you could show these at this point.

Let parents and carers know that the item of clothing they will need for next week is some form of protective clothing, such as an apron, old shirt, gardening gloves. Make sure that everyone takes home their clean (and dry!) clothing.

2

The Project

Who is going to do it?

How is it going to be done?

When is it going to be done?

Where is it going to be done?

What is needed to make it happen?

What will it cost?

How will you know if it has been successful?

Jeremiah the potter

Part one
On the peg

01 Welcome

Greet each child personally, reminding parents and carers that they are welcome to come ten minutes early to see this week's 'Showtime'. Draw attention to the coat stand or the hanger where the 'Big Cloth' is hanging. Children may have come in sophisticated protective clothing such as a fire officer's uniform (see front cover!) or with shin pads, cycle helmet, gloves, apron, overalls) so there will be lots to admire. All children will need some protective cover for their clay-work.

Make sure any new child has been given or made a badge.

If you have decided to make the Big Cloth (see page 7), explain what this is to any new children or to those who have forgotten. Any child who has brought something to put on the cloth should do so early on in the session as other children arrive. Have you added the painted rags from the last session?

02 Games/Construction
15–20 minutes

You will need
- quick-dry clay (available from craft shops)
- plastic knives and other implements for moulding
- sheets of card as a base for finished models
- plastic bags to transport home
- card for labelling and displaying
- clean-up and cover-up equipment

Give each child a piece of clay and encourage them to create whatever they like. You could suggest that they make an animal shape – do the children remember the story of Noah from the first session? Explain that their model will be on display in 'Showtime' and they will need to give

it a name, and label such as 'Henry the Hippo' or 'Jane's Jumbo'.

As an alternative you could use play dough or salt dough, but this is associated with young children and is less effective and fun. (There is a recipe for dough on page 58.)

Part two
Look in the mirror

01 Tell the story
5 minutes

You will need
- a large block of clay, enough to shape into a pot, protective floor covering and clothing and/or the *Dress Rehearsal* DVD

The DVD material for today's story is intentionally more reflective to allow the children to think about the strong visual image that God uses in the passage.

Before the session, make sure you work the clay, so that it is easy to manipulate when you come to use it in the story. Then hide the clay until you are ready. Make a show of putting on your protective clothing and sit round in a circle, with the children as close to you as possible. Talk about how important protective clothing is, including goalkeepers' gloves, cycling jackets or cricket helmets. Invite the children to imagine they are coming with you to the home of a craftsman, along with Jeremiah the prophet.

Explain who Jeremiah is – he is God's messenger sent to speak God's message to God's people living in Jerusalem. The trouble was that the people had long forgotten how to listen to God. They had not obeyed God in the way that God had wanted when Moses gave the people God's Ten Commandments. Remind the children of the last session. Jeremiah told the people how God wanted them to live. They needed to listen

Session 3

At the potter's house
Jeremiah 18:1–13,18; 31:31–34
(Into the Bible R44, R45)

Aims
To hear how Jeremiah went to the potter's shop and discovered that God has the power to shape people just as a potter shapes his pots.

To discover that God promised to be faithful to his people.

Clothes
Protective clothing

Notes for you
A child's world: Some children find it difficult to trust others and may find it hard to accept that anyone, including God, would keep their promise. But God made a clear agreement with his people which Jeremiah spoke out. Bear this in mind as you look at Jeremiah 31. This is a more abstract session, since God is promising to write his laws on people's hearts and minds. In other words, it is possible for everyone to really know God, and so it is possible for everyone to be forgiven. Only in the New Testament does it become clear that this is a message not just for the Jews. Before the session, work out how you will explain this to the children, especially those who are not part of the church community. **Top tips on Explaining the cross to children and young people** (SU 978 184227 330 0) will help you with this.

3

Words from the prompter

The 'creative medium' used in this session is clay. Children enjoy making models and using clay. As you make models together, you will have time to talk with them and build good relationships. Working with clay can take a long time and it helps if the models have begun to dry a little before being taken home. So it is suggested that the games and construction times are joined together this session and happen early on, before the children explore the story of Jeremiah. This will also enable them to think about their own experiences with clay as they hear the story.

In 'Showtime' the models can be put on display. Make sure that each is labelled and given a title, if at all possible.

and obey. But they laughed at him. It was really tough for Jeremiah. Now show the DVD or go on to tell the story like this:

Then one day, God told him to go to a potter's workshop. Jeremiah admired what the potter was making. (At this point take out the block of clay and begin shaping it into a pot. Ask the children to help. Talk about what they had done earlier.) But he noticed that sometimes the shape was not quite right. (At this point pull your pot into a funny shape.) What do you do, if it goes wrong? (Dramatically beat down the pot and start again!)

And God gave Jeremiah a message to tell the people. God had the power to protect people and to help them to be the sort of people he wanted them to be. He also had the power (like the potter) to destroy. He did not want to punish the people but he wanted them to listen and to obey. They had not been listening and doing what was right. They had been treating poor people badly. They had been worshipping other gods. God was not pleased with them! He would punish them if they did not change their behaviour.

Comment on the finished pot and say that you will show it in 'Showtime'. Can you think of a name for it? Write a suitable label.

🄯2 Bible and me
10 minutes

You will need
- copies of Jeremiah 31:31–34, Bibles or *Into the Bible* book R45
- a large piece of play dough in the shape of a heart (you could use clay, but play dough will be easier to write in – a play dough recipe is on page 58), stick to 'write' with

Explain that later, God gave Jeremiah another message to God's people. This time it was a promise of hope, a new agreement. Ask the children to look out for what God will do. Either they can read it in small groups or ask them just to listen as you read.

Take the stick and ask a child to write on the play dough what God said he will do. You will need to agree the exact words such as, 'God will be their God' and, 'God will forgive their sins'. Ask what the children think this means and explain it in child-friendly language.

God was promising to be especially close to his people. Each person would have God's law written on their heart (although not literally). Each person can know God! Wow! What's more,

he promised to forgive them. God always keeps his promises.

The heart could also go on display for 'Showtime'.

🄯3 Learn and remember
5 minutes

This new Learn and remember verse comes from Jeremiah 31. To help the children to learn it, work out some signs together, which you can do as you say the verse:

🌀 *God said, "I will be their God and they will be my people."* 🌀
Jeremiah 31:33

Your verse signs could look like this: God said, "I will be their God (Put up three fingers, wrap the other hand round them and then move that hand upwards towards the ceiling – God is three in one.) and they (Move an open flat hand away from you as though displaying something – everyone.) will be my people. (Fold hands over chest as though 'mine')" Jeremiah 31:33 (Write J on one palm with the index finger of the other hand, then on the palm, place three fingers and one finger, followed by three fingers and three fingers to indicate 31 and 33.)

Go on to the *Dress Rehearsal* website to see pictures of possible signs to use with this verse.

Share an occasion when you have known that you belong to God.

🄯4 Conversation with God
5 minutes

Each child brings or wears their protective clothing and talks together about how these clothes protect them from different dangers or damage. Comment on the overalls needed for making the clay models. Introduce the idea that you are now coming to talk with God, who is often referred to as a protector, the one who is always with us and committed to our well-being. Remind them of the picture of God as an eagle from the last session. Because God is like this, we can speak with him, confident that he will hear, understand and act.

Ask the children to then find a place in the room where they are comfortable. It might be near a window, near a person, in a corner or on a chair. You may be surprised how the children respond. Encourage them to close their eyes. You are introducing a time of silent reflection.

Ask them to imagine they are a heart made

out of clay. (You are not asking them to answer out loud any of the questions you are asking.) Imagine God is writing on them how much he loves them and wants them to belong to him. How does that make them feel?

But now imagine that they cannot quite see what he has written. They have done something which is stopping them from seeing his message to them. Maybe it is something they have said or done wrong. Ask them if there is anything they want to tell God about that they know has displeased him. Remind them that God has promised to 'forgive their sins and forget the evil things they have done.' Remind them that God keeps his promises.

Finally, they can now see the heart. What name is God calling them? In return, what do they want to say to God who knows them by name? When they are ready, invite them to open their eyes.

Part three
Ready to go on stage

31 Preparing for 'Showtime'
15 minutes

Display the clay models and the play dough heart you have made on a table, including the names of the potter and the title given to each 'creation'.

Showtime

Welcome parents and carers as they arrive and let them admire the clay creations. (Only dismantle the display when everyone has had a chance to see it.) Ask them to sit down before you show the signs for the Learn and remember verse. If appropriate, find out how the community project is going. Advise the adults that for the next session children will need to bring something to protect their heads from the sun since they are going on a picnic. Assure parents that the children will not be eating very much.

Session 4

Jesus feeds the crowd
John 6:1–13
(Into the Bible R82)

Aims

To hear about the time when Jesus fed over 5,000 people and provided for them in practical ways.

To recognise that Jesus cares for us too.

Clothes
A sun hat

Notes for you

A child's world: In this story, it appears that Jesus is doing something magical, 'bringing more and more rabbits out of a hat'. Of course, it was nothing of the sort because this was no trick, but another example of Jesus meeting the needs of those who flocked to him. He did this because he is God.

This session emphasises the fact that Jesus saw the needs of the crowd and was able to meet them. This story will be known to some of the children but this is the first time in **Dress Rehearsal** that Jesus has been introduced. Encourage children to think about their needs and to understand that they can ask Jesus to help them. Of course, he may not do what they expect, but then, the disciples did not expect Jesus to feed the crowd either!

Feeding over 5,000

Part one
On the peg

01 Welcome

Greet each child personally, reminding parents and carers that they are welcome to come ten minutes early to join in this week's 'Showtime'. Draw attention to the coat stand or the hanger where the 'Big Cloth' is hanging. Any child who has brought something to put on the cloth should do so early on in the session, as other children arrive.

Give some sort of headgear to any child who comes without a sun hat.

01 Games
10 minutes

You will need
- props for team games that develop the picnic theme

Play one or two games that are themed around food. Here are a few suggestions; there are more games in *Ultimate Games* (SU 978 184427 365 2).
- Label the four walls of the room with the names of picnic food such as sandwiches, crisps, fruit and sausage rolls. Call out one of the names – the children should run and touch that wall as quickly as they can. The last person and the last but one has to sit out for two goes. When you call out, 'It's going to rain' everyone has to run to touch all four walls.
- Make several copies of pictures of ten picnic foods. Scatter them around the room and challenge teams of children to find a full set
- Play a variation of 'What's the time, Mr Wolf' and when the wolf says, 'Picnic time!' everyone has to run back to base.

Part two
Look in the mirror

21 Tell the story
5 minutes

You will need
- the story 'And the rest…' from page 30 of *The 10 Must Know Stories* or from page 54, and/or episode 4 in the *Dress Rehearsal* DVD

After reading the story or seeing the DVD episode, talk about what it was like for Nat (or the boy with the loaves) at the various points of the story.

22 Bible and me
5 minutes

You will need
- sun hats
- copies of John 6:5–13 or part of R82 from *Into the Bible*
- a bread roll and a tin of tuna

Ask the children to imagine a crowd that is at least 25 times the size of their school. Where would you put them all?

Imagine being in that crowd, the sun has been hot all day, you are hungry, it is time to go home but there is a long way to walk. How would you feel? (Everyone wears their sunhats.)

Ask them to imagine how much food you would need to feed a crowd that size. (Show them the bread roll and talk about how many supermarket trolleys you would need. Then show the group the tin of tuna, enough to feed four people.) What about over 1,000 times more than four people? How many supermarket trolleys would that be?

And Jesus fed them all! Ask the children to read John 6:5–13 or read the story as a play script from *Into the Bible*.

Ask if the people, including the disciples, expected Jesus to help? (They did not ask him because they just did not expect him to help.)

Ask why Jesus performed this miracle. (He saw and cared for people who were hungry. And because he was God, he was able to help them.)

Ask how much food was left over. (The equivalent of 12 trolleys!) Marvel at how extraordinary this was.

Comment that Jesus cares for us and he can do far more than we ever expect. (You could give a personal example.)

2 3 Conversation with God
5 minutes

You will need
- a paper plate for everyone
- felt-tip pens
- one large sticky label per child with the words 'God has heard' written on it

Encourage each child to write their name on the back of the plate. Ask the group to think of something that they really need that God could help them with. Make suggestions such as something difficult at school, a need in their family. (Try to avoid yet more games or clothes!) At the centre of the plate, ask them to write or draw what the need is, but encourage them to keep their writing or drawing small.

Sitting in a circle, each child should hold out their plate and in the silence talk to God about their need. Then give out the sticky labels and show the group how to stick the label over what they have written or drawn. This means that what the child has written/drawn is a secret between them and God. Assure the children that Jesus knows what we need but he wants us to talk with him.

2 4 Learn and remember
5 minutes

You will need
- the signs you worked out for this promise of God from last session

⑤ God said, "I will be their God and they will be my people." ⑤
Jeremiah 31:33

Briefly remind the children of this verse by going over the signs from last week. To reinforce it, the verse splits into 15 words (keeping the chapter and verse as one). Give each word to a child (you may have to give each child more than one word). The children should stand up in turn, say their word and then sit down. Do this more than once.

Comment that God made this promise to Jeremiah over 500 years before Jesus was born. But Jesus came to make it possible for all people to really know God and to belong to him. This miracle was a sign that Jesus had come from God and indeed, was God.

Part three
Ready to go on stage

③ 1 Preparing for 'Showtime'
15 or more minutes

(Do this earlier in the session if you are going to cook food, such as biscuits or pizza.)

Tailor the food you make to suit the group, the time of day, your facilities and your budget. 'Picnic food' can mean any number of things, so you should be able to come up with a good range of snacks for everyone. Try to include healthy options and be aware of food allergies and health and safety constraints. To make a close link with the story you could include tuna sandwiches or tuna on savoury biscuits.

Arrange the food attractively. Open picnic boxes could be made out of card. Each parent could have a personalised serviette. Paper cups could be decorated. Read the story from page 54.

Words from the prompter
The 'creative medium' used in this session is making food. This will be attractively arranged for a picnic snack to eat when parents and carers arrive. You will re-enact the incident when Jesus fed a crowd on a hillside.

4

Showtime

Welcome parents and carers as they arrive.
Arrange them in small, clearly distinct groups on the
floor, using rugs, cushions or low chairs for those who
do not wish to sit on the floor. Explain that Jesus had been
teaching a very large crowd of over 5,000 people and
at the end of the day, they were very hungry. But instead of
sending them home hungry, what did he do? Ask the children to tell
everyone the story. Explain that is what you are going to do.

Give thanks to God for the food which has already been
provided (in other words, this is no miracle), then use adult helpers to give
out food so that children don't have to wait to eat. Children should use the
paper plates they had in Conversation with God. (It is better to serve people
than to ask them to come to a central serving point, since that is more
authentic to the original story.)

At the end, comment on how much or how little has been left over.
Make the connection with what happened in Jesus' miracle. Remind the
children that Jesus knows what we need and we can talk with him about it.

Advise the adults that for the next session children will need to bring
a sling or a piece of plaster or bandage.

The good Samaritan

Session 5

Who is your neighbour?
Luke 10:25–37
(Into the Bible R75)

Aims
To explore the story of the good Samaritan.

To recognise that God's people love God with everything they have, which leads them to love others too!

Clothes
Bandage, plaster or sling

Part one
On the peg

01 Welcome

Greet each child personally, reminding parents and carers that they are welcome to come ten minutes early to see this week's 'Showtime'. Draw attention to the coat stand or the hanger where the 'Big Cloth' is hanging. Any child who has brought something to put on the cloth should do so early on in the session, as other children arrive.

Make sure any new child has been given or made a badge.

Admire the slings and bandages that children have brought and wrap a small piece of bandage around anyone who has not brought anything. Remember that some people are allergic to plasters.

02 Games
10 minutes

You will need
• props for team games including material for a sling for each team

Devise a series of team races that assume that people only have use of one arm because their other one is in a sling or only the use of one leg because their other leg is bandaged. Be sensitive to anyone with genuine disabilities. The games could include: a three-legged race, a one-handed egg and spoon race, hopping, wheelbarrow race, batting a balloon along the ground with only one hand, putting a hat and scarf on with one hand to run to a set point and back and then take them off to pass to the next in the team (surprisingly difficult!). Make sure that your teams are mixed ability.

Comment on the fact that we need to support those who have some form of disability.

Part two
Look in the mirror

21 Bible and me
10 minutes

You will need
• Bibles or R75 from *Into the Bible*

'Bible and me' comes before 'Tell the story' this session because it introduces the story.

Ask three confident readers to read Luke 10:25–29, taking the parts of the narrator, Jesus and the expert in the Law of Moses. (It would help if they have practised beforehand.) Introduce the three readers in their roles but before they read, ask the children to think of one way they might think to describe the expert. For example, is he interested in what Jesus has to say? Does he want to trick Jesus? Is he proud? After the children have listened, see what they think about the expert.

Say that you have three questions to ask the children. You want to know what they think.
• What did the expert want to know that he had to do? What does that mean? (Eternal life means having a relationship with God, now and for ever.) Comment at this stage that he was committed to keeping all the laws of Moses, and there were lots of them. He thought this would be enough to please God!
• What did Jesus say the man had to do to please God?
• What did Jesus say the man had to do about others? What is a neighbour? (You will get several answers. Don't try to correct them for you will be returning to this question. Say that Jesus went on to tell a story to explain what he meant by a neighbour.)

Notes for you
A child's world:
Children want to please others, which during this club may mean you as a leader! That is a natural response. As leaders you need to give praise generously, without singling out one child for special approval.

The expert in the Law wanted to catch Jesus out. As a Jewish leader, he was committed to keeping all the Jewish laws in their minute detail which he thought was how God wanted him to live. But Jesus suggested that knowing God and being sure of life with him (both now and to eternity) was not about keeping laws. It was all about believing – loving God with everything he had and loving his neighbour. God's approval comes without conditions attached. This was so very different. The challenge of the story of the good Samaritan is that God does not require us to keep lots of laws, but simply to love him deeply ⟫

5

and to love others, however demanding that might be.

Children will appreciate a story about the posh and important who don't behave with compassion. Make sure they have grasped that the Samaritan was someone whom Jesus' listeners would have looked down on. Think too about how you will explain 'eternal life'. The definition used in **Dress Rehearsal** is 'Being with God and knowing he is with us, now and for ever'. God loves us unconditionally and wants us to spend all of our lives for ever with him, beginning from now. It is more about the quality of living than the length of time we spend with him beyond death!

Words from the prompter

The 'creative medium' used in this session is mime. The story has a simple storyline but plenty of emotion. Don't worry if you are not experienced in doing drama with children. Yours is not a professional performance and the children will probably help you. Don't force any child to join in who doesn't want to.

2 Tell the story *5 minutes*

You will need
• a copy of 'The good Samaritan' from *The 10 Must Know Stories* (or from page 55), and/or episode 5 from the Dress Rehearsal DVD

(The story 'The good Samaritan' is an unusual version and one that is much appreciated by children who warm to Larry the lizard!)

After reading the story or seeing the DVD episode, check that children appreciate how much the Jews (who were listening to Jesus) disliked the Samaritans. Tell the children that the Jewish law said that no one should touch a dead body, so the first two men on the road were actually keeping the law (because the injured man might have been dead) but by keeping the law they were not helping someone in need. Was it difficult or easy to love a neighbour? Would the children like to change their definition of a neighbour from the one they came up with earlier?

Refer back to the discussion about the expert. He kept all the laws but Jesus said that being with God and knowing him, now and for ever, was not about keeping laws. It was about loving and trusting God and others. Now that was very different. We need God's help to love him as much as that and to love others. This leads on from last session's Learn and remember verse.

3 Learn and remember
5 minutes

The verse for this and the next session is:

Love the LORD your God with all your heart, soul and strength.
Deuteronomy 6:5

You could teach this as a song – one can be found on *Bitesize Bible Songs 1* (SU 978 184427 260 0) or as a download from the SU website (search for 'Deuteronomy 6:5').

You may prefer to use the version found in Luke 10:27 which reads: 'Love the Lord your God with all your heart, soul, strength, and mind.' You could also add the second part: 'Love your neighbours as much as you love yourself.'

You could use four signs for 'heart', 'soul', 'strength' and 'mind'. For 'soul' the sign could be closing the eyes tightly to concentrate on what is deep within you, that which communicates with God.

4 Conversation with God
5 minutes

You will need
• a sticky label that looks like sticking plaster
• pen

The good Samaritan showed that he cared for the man even though he may not have liked him. Just as was the case for the first two men, it was very inconvenient for him and dangerous. But he was doing what pleased God! Given a choice, this was more important than keeping all the laws of Moses. The first two men were not good neighbours. God will help us to do what is hard.

In the prayer-time, the children will pray for someone they could be a good neighbour to. This may be someone who is ill or someone most people don't like. Ask the children to write or draw on their sticky label the person they want to ask God to help. They then stick the label on their arm. (You could use actual sticking plaster for this, but you will need to check before the session that no children are allergic to it.)

Draw this time to a close by asking God to help you all to be good neighbours even though it may be tough. The label will remind the children to pray for this person and to be kind to others.

4 Construction

You will need
• material to make something for someone in need

Before the session, choose something that you could all make to give to someone who is in need. This could be a card for someone sick, a glass jar decorated with glass paint, a bookmark made by decorating a peg, a finger puppet. There are plenty of other ideas in *Ultimate Craft* (SU 978 184427 364 5). As you work, chat with the children about the story and what they thought. Or you could chat generally to carry on building your relationships.

Part three
Ready to go on stage

91 Preparing for 'Showtime'
15 minutes

There are ten parts in this version of the story: a narrator, Larry who speaks and Larry who mimes, two robbers, the injured man, three travellers and the owner of the guest house. But this could be extended by having other robbers, more lizards and other people at the guest house. You could also have a donkey or two and large rocks. Other children could make sound effects. Essentially, as the story is read, you want the children to play their parts. Make use of an aisle or whatever space you have so that those travelling have as much floor space to cover as possible. Explain to the children the direction they come from and go to, the locations of the lizard's rock and the guest house. Two rehearsals should be sufficient.

Ask each child to imagine how their person would feel and what expressions would be on their face as the story unfolds. Insist that there is no violence! Simple props would help such as an eye patch, bag, money, smart hat.

As an alternative, tell this story using puppets but that would require more preparation unless you already have a set of puppets and some expertise.

Showtime

Welcome parents and carers as they arrive. When they are all seated, introduce the story by saying that an expert in the Jewish law who was very good at keeping the law in detail, came to trick Jesus. He wanted to know what exactly he had to do to keep the law to be sure that God accepted him. Jesus said it was not about keeping every law; it was more about really loving God and loving others. This expert was not satisfied with this answer. He asked a follow-up question: 'Who is my neighbour?' In reply, Jesus told this story, well, not quite like this, but almost…

Show the mime, taking as long as you can, with children coming down the aisle, going across the 'stage' at a suitable pace and making the most of the drama.

Advise the adults that for the next session the children will need to bring an old pair of shoes or if they cannot do this, some old clothes. They do not necessarily have to wear their old shoes, just bring them!

Session 6

The prodigal son
Luke 15:11–32
(Into the Bible R77)

Aims
To explore the story of the son who went away, the son who stayed and the father who welcomed them both.

To explore how much God loves and forgives those who come to him.

Clothes
Old shoes or old clothes

Notes for you
A child's world:
Children long to be loved and accepted if they mess things up. The teachers and experts of the law (remember last session!) were in the audience listening to Jesus' story. They resented the fact that he said that keeping the law did not guarantee God's acceptance but that it was how people responded to God that mattered. The story of the prodigal son may be known by many children, at least the first part. It is a powerful tale of a son who returns repentant to his father and is accepted back. So it is with God, who accepts us as we are, because he loves us and wants us to belong to him. But there is also the elder son who has done the right thing and resents his father's forgiveness of his brother – just as the experts of the law resented the outsiders and those who were not Jews.

You will be able to emphasise that ➡

The tale of two sons

Part one
On the peg

01 Welcome

Greet each child personally, reminding parents and carers that they are welcome to come ten minutes early to see this week's 'Showtime'. Draw attention to the coat stand or the hanger where the 'Big Cloth' is hanging. Any child who has brought something to put on the cloth should do so early on in the session, as other children arrive.

Make sure any new child has been given or made a badge.

Any child who arrives without old shoes or clothes should be given something old, with a hole in. Children do not necessarily have to wear their old shoes or clothes, just bring them!

02 Games
10 minutes

You will need
• parachute

Gather the children around the edge of the parachute and show them how to lift it up into a mushroom – all the players lift the parachute high in the air so that it balloons up in the middle. Number the children 1, 2 and 3 and ask all the number 1s to take off one shoe and throw it under the parachute. Lift and lower the chute twice and then on the third time lift it into a mushroom. The number 1s should run underneath and retrieve their shoe from the middle. If they are caught under the chute when it descends, then they should return their shoe to the middle and go again with the number 2s. Play until everyone has had a go.

This game is taken from *Ultimate Games* (SU 978 184427 365 2), where more shoe games are available!

Part two
Look in the mirror

21 Tell the story
5 minutes

You will need
• 'The Tale of Two Sons' from page 39 of *The 10 Must Know Stories* or from page 56, and/or episode 6 from the *Dress Rehearsal* DVD

If you are reading the story from page 56, ask the children to stand up every time they hear the word 'shoes'. (The original story has been amended to accommodate the shoe theme.) Alternatively, three leaders could act out the parts. This will enable the children to see the difference in the facial expressions of the two sons.

After hearing or watching the story, talk about the different feelings of the two sons and their father as the story progressed. Tell the children that it was a disgraceful thing for a Jew to keep pigs, which showed just how desperate the son was. Working for his father was a better thing to do but he did not expect to be forgiven and accepted back as a son.

Wonder with the children why the older son was so unwelcoming. Remind them that the experts in the Law of Moses that you came across last week were listening carefully to Jesus' story. They knew Jesus was saying that they were like the older son. How might that be?

⚫2 Bible and me
5 minutes

You will need

- Bibles or copies of *Into the Bible* (R77), flip chart with two columns labelled 'Surprised Father' and 'Surprised Son'

Read Luke 15:20–24 out loud or ask the children to read the passage in small groups (with adult help).

Ask the children to help you fill in the two columns:

- What was is that surprised the father? (His son came home, his son wanted to be just a worker.)
- What was it that surprised the son? (His father welcomed him; his father gave him a party and new clothes.)
- Ask why the father was able to welcome the son back.
- Explain that in the same way, God loves us and welcomes us, wanting the best for us, if only we ask him. He was really happy.
- Comment on how unhappy the older son was.

⚫3 Learn and remember
5 minutes

You will need

- a jumbled up version of Deuteronomy 6:5 (or the fuller version in Luke 10 if that is what you used last session): "**Love the Lord your God with all your heart, soul and strength.**"

Jumbled up this could read:

🔄 *Evol the Rold your Dog with lal your herat, lous and grentsth.* 🔄
Deuteryonom 6:5

Show this and ask the children to unravel it. Remind them that the experts in the Law of Moses thought that as long as they were careful to keep the law they would be accepted by God. Jesus told them that that was not enough. God wanted them to know he loved them and wanted to forgive them. The younger son realised that only too well!

⚫4 Conversation with God
5 minutes

You will need

- a shoe with eight eyelets for laces (this could be either a cardboard outline or a real lace-up shoe – a large clown's shoe would be ideal), a long lace or thick coloured wool

Talk about shoelaces and ask how many children have any shoes with laces that need tying. (Even Olympic athletes run with laces undone!) Explain that you are going to lace up this shoe and each time the lace goes through an eyelet, you are going to say something to God.

Just before you thread the lace through the first four eyelets, ask for a suggestion of something we want to say sorry to God about. Then as you thread through the last four, ask for suggestions for what God says to us when we say sorry. You will need to have some ideas to help the children, such as, 'I forgive you!', 'Welcome', 'I love you'.

Part three
Ready to go on stage

🔼1 Preparing for 'Showtime'/Construction
15 minutes

You will need

- long strips of paper (or one large long strip, such as a piece of lining paper or old wallpaper)
- art materials
- small boxes that can be turned into televisions (or one large box); or digital camera and computer with PowerPoint (or other presentation software)

Encourage the children to draw the following scenes on their long strip of paper (or work together on one large version). Sandals are difficult to draw so assure children it is OK to draw shoes if they wish.

1 The son leaves, wearing an ordinary shoe/ sandal. He might even have a spare pair on view hanging out of the top of his bag.
2 The son wears some very bright shoes while he is having a party.
3 His shoes are full of holes while he looks after the pigs.
4 He walks home barefoot.
5 His father gives him a brand new pair of shoes.
6 His brother is wearing heavy working boots.

Decorate the box like a television and cut a slit at either side of the box. Feed the paper through the slot and move the 'film strip' through the television as you tell the story.

There are two versions of these model televisions in *Ultimate Craft* (SU 978 184427 364 5).

➡️ God loves and accepts us as we are if we come to him. You can also reinforce the message that God's longing for us to love him and obey him is far more important than doing what seems right, as was discovered in previous sessions.

Words from the prompter
The 'creative medium' used in this session is art or photography. You will create a 'roll of film' of the story focusing upon feet and footwear. This is either done by drawing a series of scenes on a long strip of paper and threading that strip through a box made to look like a television. A large version could be used in 'Showtime' to tell the story. Alternatively, you can create a series of tableaux that tell the story, photograph them digitally and present them in PowerPoint.

6

Alternatively, work with the children to come up with tableaux (frozen scenes where the children take the parts of the characters) that show each of the above scenes. Take photographs of the scenes and display them using PowerPoint (or using other presentation software). Show the photographs as you tell the story.

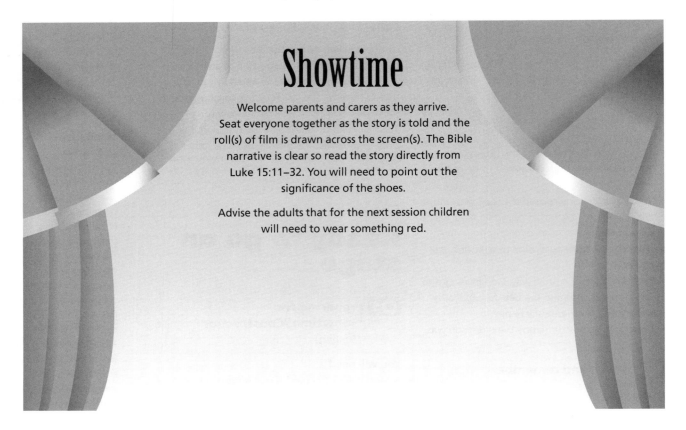

Showtime

Welcome parents and carers as they arrive. Seat everyone together as the story is told and the roll(s) of film is drawn across the screen(s). The Bible narrative is clear so read the story directly from Luke 15:11–32. You will need to point out the significance of the shoes.

Advise the adults that for the next session children will need to wear something red.

Jesus' trial

Session 7

Jesus goes before his accusers
Matthew 27:15–26,27–32;
28:1–10
(**Into the Bible** R58, R59, R61)

Aims
To explore the trial of Jesus and his death that then leads on to his resurrection.

To help children reflect on Jesus' trial especially, and then his resurrection and what it might mean for them.

Clothes
Something red

Part one
On the peg

01 Welcome

Greet each child personally, reminding parents and carers that they are welcome to come ten minutes early to see this week's 'Showtime'. Draw attention to the coat stand or the hanger where the 'Big Cloth' is hanging. Any child who has brought something to put on the cloth should do so early on in the session, as other children arrive. You may intend to add lots of images to this in the construction time.

Any child who arrives without something red can be given a red sticker or red ribbon to wear around their wrist.

02 Games
10 minutes

You will need
• props for games that make use of anything red

For your games this session, adapt some popular games to include the colour red. These could include passing a red balloon or ball along a line of children, fishing small balls from a ball pond with extra points for red ones, using red scarves for a three-legged race, asking children to perform a specific task (such as running to touch three walls, hopping ten times on the spot) if they are wearing a certain colour – when you choose the colour red, everyone should perform the task.

Part two
Look in the mirror

21 Tell the story
10 minutes

You will need
• a red/scarlet coat or piece of cloth
• Bibles or copies of *Into the Bible* (R58, R59, R61)
• adult helpers to act out Matthew 27:15–26 (R58) as you read it
• episode 7 from the *Dress Rehearsal DVD*

If you are reading the story, you will need actors to mime the part of Jesus, Barabbas, Pilate, at least two chief priests and the children are to be the crowd. You might also want Pilate's wife to appear. Write the words 'Nail him to a cross!' and 'Barabbas' and possibly 'We and our own families will take the blame for his death' on pieces of card to show the children what they have to shout out when they see each card. Dress up as much as you can, since dressing up is a key part of *Dress Rehearsal!*

The narrator needs to read slowly and, if necessary, add in extra detail such as explaining what the Passover is, or checking that the children know who Jesus, the chief priests and the leaders are. Remind the children that only a few days earlier, this same crowd had been welcoming Jesus as their king as he rode into Jerusalem on a donkey. Children ought to remain seated as members of the crowd to ensure things don't get out of hand but do encourage them to shout and boo. (If you want the children to play a fuller part, you will need to have practised beforehand.)

As you read Matthew 27:27–32 (R59) and Jesus is led away, wrap a scarlet/red coat or piece of cloth around Jesus.

Afterwards, split into small groups, each with a leader, to explore the following questions:

Notes for you
A child's world: Last session introduced the idea of the father who loved his rebellious son and accepted him back. This is preparation for the story of Jesus' trial which leads to his death. Jesus' death made it possible for God the father to forgive us for the wrong that we do. The story of the crucifixion is long and violent. It is central to what we believe as Christians, although without the resurrection it is a story of despair and failure. The actual crucifixion story (Matthew 27:33–44 and R60) is not used in this outline, although it would be great to retell that story to the children if you can. To explore different ways to explain the meaning of the cross at a deeper level, get hold of a copy of **Top Tips on Explaining the cross to children and young people** (SU 978 184427 330 0).

7

➜ The emphasis that is taken on the story of the trial and resurrection as told in these passages from Matthew has four main points:

- Jesus was treated unjustly but was not a failure
- Barabbas was saved in place of Jesus
- Jesus died
- Jesus came alive again two days later

It is important that children grasp these points as far as they are able.

Words from the prompter

The 'creative medium' used in this session is collage-making. This will be in two parts: images from the scene of the trial using the colours red and black, and images from the garden scene using bright yellow and green. This could be on a material banner, a large poster, individual posters or could be added to the 'Big Cloth'. These are to be displayed during 'Showtime'

Note that for colour-blind children the colours red and green are often the colours that get confused.

There may be some children who want to know more about what it means to be a friend of Jesus, to recognise that God can forgive us because of what Jesus has done in dying on the cross. Be prepared for this. The booklets **Jesus= friendship forever, Me+Jesus** and **Friends with Jesus** are very suitable to use with children aged 10 to 12, 8 to 10 and 5 to 8 respectively. For more details see page 13.

- What did Jesus do, throughout the trial? (Stood there and made no comment.)
- Why did Pilate find it so difficult to make up his mind?
- What did the chief priests and leaders want to happen?
- What did the crowd want?
- How did the children feel being in the crowd as the story was told?
- How did they feel shouting against Jesus in the crowd? (This last question may puzzle the children but encourage older children to think about this.)
- Was it fair or unfair for Jesus to die? Try to ask for a reason for each answer given. Briefly explore the injustice of Jesus' trial. Ask how Barabbas might have felt. Allow time for the children to put themselves in Barabbas' shoes. (This will be hard for boys to do, so give them time to think and be understanding if they don't come up with an answer.)
- If possible, ask the children what they had learned to like about Jesus in the last few sessions.

❷❷ Bible and me
5 minutes

You will need
- Bibles or copies of *Into the Bible* (R61)
- the red coat/cloth from 'Tell the story'

You can either do this in the same small groups or all together. The competence of your small group leaders may help you choose what to do.

Explain that the red cloth stands for the red/scarlet robe that was put around Jesus' shoulders as the soldiers laughed at him. It may have been a coat that a Roman soldier wore but red was also a sign of a king. The soldiers did not respect Jesus at all and in no way did they treat him as a king.

Ask what the colour red also stands for (children might suggest Manchester United or Arsenal but look for the answer 'blood'). Jesus really did die and blood gushed out of his side. He was buried in a tomb, late Friday afternoon and a huge stone was rolled over the entrance. Early on the Sunday morning, some of his friends came to see his body to put perfume beside it.

Either ask the children to listen out for the following two things in Matthew 28:1–10 (R61), or if appropriate ask them to read for themselves: something that shocked the women and something that made them feel happy.

Talk about their observations. Explain that Jesus

had indeed died, and this was part of God's plan. It was not an accident. He had died in place of Barabbas, taking the blame for his wrongdoing.

Explain that one way of understanding Jesus' death is to see that he died in place of every person who has ever lived. He took the blame for the wrong we have done. Because of that, we can be forgiven if we say sorry, just like the father forgave his son in the story of the two sons from the last session.

Share how important it is to you that Jesus is alive now. Jesus came alive again to show that the wrong things have been dealt with.

❷❸ Learn and remember
5 minutes

Say Matthew 28:6 to the children twice and then work out signs for the key phrases.

🖐️ *Jesus isn't here! God has raised him to life.* ✋
Matthew 28:6

You will need to remind the children of the context. 'Jesus' could be pointing at a nail print in each palm. The children will make other suggestions.

❷❹ Conversation with God
5 minutes

You have a choice of two ways of praying:

■ JESUS' DEATH

You will need
- two small sticks (either twigs or lollipop sticks)
- a strip of red cloth

Show the children how to bind their two sticks together to make a cross by wrapping the red cloth around the cross. Each child should then find a quiet space and sit cross-legged, holding their cross. Ask them to think about the sad story of Jesus' trial and death. Barabbas deserved to die but Jesus died in his place and took the blame for the wrong Barabbas had done. But Jesus also died for us, to take the blame for all the wrongs things we have done that God has not wanted us to do. Ask them to think of things they have done that they know have displeased God. After a short pause, thank God that Jesus did die and wants to forgive us. Then ask any child who wants to know more about being God's friend to come to see you or one of the other leaders afterwards.

■ **JESUS IS ALIVE TODAY!**

You will need
- chalk or a long piece of rope
- cards labelled with places where children might be sad or afraid

Create a large circle on the floor with chalk or rope. (With a large group, you will need more than one circle.) Inside the circle, place a sign for 'school', 'playground', 'travelling', swimming pool', 'shops', 'somewhere else', places where a child might be afraid or sad. (You could draw a sad mouth with chalk underneath the sign.) Ask the children to stand in one of these places or if they cannot think of anywhere specific, in the 'somewhere else' place.

Remind the children that the women were afraid in the garden but then they heard that Jesus was alive, and even better, they met him! Their fear turned to happiness. As they stand in their sad place, ask them to imagine they are there but then to remember that Jesus is alive and with them. Pray out loud, asking God to help each child to know that Jesus is alive and with us in sad places where we might be afraid. (Change the chalk sad mouth to a chalk happy mouth.) Invite any child with sad thoughts to share with a leader after the session if they would like to.

Part three
Ready to go on stage

91 **Preparing for 'Showtime'/Construction**
15 minutes

You will need
- plain material or paper
- glue
- stapler
- variety of fabric or types of paper coloured red, black, green and yellow, coloured magazine pages

Before the session, decide whether you are going to make one large or several smaller individual or small-group collages, using the colours red and black for the trial and death of Jesus, and green and yellow for the resurrection scene in the garden.

Set the children the task of creating two images, using the materials you have provided. This could be done by coming up with one shape or object that represents the story of Jesus' trial and one that represents him coming alive again. They could cut out lots of squares from a magazine and make a paper mosaic of a cross. They could make a cross shape or a stone from the tomb out of black tissue paper or felt, or drops of blood from red foil, or twisted red material for the cloak, or dried flowers twisted into a smile. Make some examples to inspire ideas.

Allow plenty of time, but if some children are finding it hard or are not interested suggest that they help you cover a display board (or whatever you are going to use) to display the collages. Throughout this time, talk with the children about the story. Leaders should also be making a collage unless they need to help the children.

7

Showtime

Welcome parents and carers as they arrive.
Present the story of Jesus' trial as you have done it earlier.
If you have only watched the DVD, you could present it
as suggested above, but only expect the children to join in.
Then explain to the adults what the children have done and
admire the collages together.

Advise adults that for the next session children need to wear something
suitable for a wedding. It should not be a complete wedding outfit –
something like a bow tie or ribbon is quite sufficient. Explain too that there
is going to be a wedding banquet. Make this clear if you need extra helpers
or if adults are going to be invited to join in.

If parents and carers are going to be invited to the whole of the
wedding banquet, children could create invitations or posters during
the session and give them out here.

The end of time

Session 8

The new Jerusalem
Revelation 21:1–6; 22:1–5
(**Into the Bible** R101)

Aims
To explore what the Bible says about the end of time.

To celebrate the end of the Dress Rehearsal **programme.**

Clothes
Wedding clothes

Part one
On the peg

01 Welcome

Greet each child personally, reminding parents and carers that they are welcome to come ten minutes early to join in the final 'Showtime'. If parents and carers are present for the whole session, let them know what is planned and give them a special welcome. Admire the wedding clothes that children have come in and give any child who has forgotten or not got any 'best' clothes, a piece of tinsel to wear in their hair (for girls) or a flower buttonhole.

The 'Big Cloth' should be on display unless you intend to complete it in the course of the session.

The following activities should happen in the order that best suits your group, though Pass the parcel is designed to lead into watching the DVD episode and reading the Bible passage.

02 Games
10 minutes

As this is the final session of *Dress Rehearsal* you may want to play the games that have worked best or been most enjoyed in the last seven sessions. Or you may want to create some new games more tightly tied to the theme.

- **Matching fruit:** create a set of cards made up of pairs of different coloured cards, each with an outline of a different half of fruit – pear, banana, apple, plum, peach, hairy gooseberry, rhubarb, orange or more exotic fruit such as Ugli fruit or kumquat. Give out one card to each child/adult and everyone has to find their identical-coloured partner. As soon as they do, they sit down. Using a stop watch, see how quickly they can do this. Then try to beat the first length of time, a second or third time round. With a small group, give out several cards so that children have to find several partners.

- **Guess the fruit:** each child/adult has a plastic cup and tastes several unmarked fruit juices, one at a time. Can they guess which fruit is which? They write down their guess on a score card, with the number of juices available in one column and space for the answers in another column. (Mixed fruit juices would be more of a challenge!)

- **Pass the parcel:** create a parcel which has an invitation inside to come to the wedding banquet. Between each layer, there could be an invitation upon which is written one of the following words: God/will/make/his home/among/his/people. Once all the layers have been unwrapped, after the music has stopped each time, the children can sort out the words into the right order. Explain that this is something that John heard in his vision which is what you will be looking at this session. This game leads into reading the Bible passage and watching the DVD episode.

Part two
Look in the mirror

21 Tell the story
10 minutes

You will need
- Bibles or copies of *Into the Bible*
- episode 8 from the *Dress Rehearsal* DVD (which very effectively opens up John's vision of what it will be like at the end of time)

Whether you are going to show the DVD or simply explore the Bible passage, introduce the theme as follows:

Remind the children of the story of when God made the world and how beautiful and perfect it all was. Those who have been part of *Showstoppers!*, the holiday club linked to this programme, will have explored the story

Notes for you
A child's world: So what is it going to be like at the end of time? When we die we do know that those who have loved Jesus will go to be with him in heaven. But what is heaven like? We don't know much and we certainly don't know where heaven is. It is not a place as we know it and not necessarily up in the sky. Children will have a strange mixture of ideas from clouds, to harps, to lakes of chocolate to cream cheese adverts. Heaven is also associated with death and maybe separation from people they love and even from pets they love too. Be aware of any pastoral situations which call for extra sensitivity.

But beyond this, there is the bigger question, which is really addressed by Revelation chapters 21 and 22 – what will happen at the end of time, when God will create a new heaven and new earth? John's vision in Revelation is of a bride (God's

41

8

⟳ people, represented as a city) coming down to earth. The new heaven and earth is full of everything that is positive and of God. This theme is very appropriate for a programme called **Dress Rehearsal**. In one sense, all of life is a dress rehearsal for what is to happen at the end of time, when those who love God will be with him for ever, part of his new creation! This is too abstract for children to grasp but if they capture but a glimpse of this great truth, you will have set them on the right path!

There are two aims for this session – to fill the children's minds (and the minds of any adults present) with the glorious hope that those who love God can have, and secondly to celebrate the end of **Dress Rehearsal**, making it clear what is planned for the following weeks and months.

You may have invited all parents and carers for the whole session. This will affect what you do, and for those who are not Christians, it is a genuine opportunity to present to them what Christians believe the Bible says will happen at the end of time. Many will have no idea of the theme to be found in Revelation 21 and 22. Be prepared to answer their questions and if you do not know the answers, make sure you can find out to let them know at a later date.

of creation in the first session. But everything began to go wrong when people decided to live life without paying attention to God. Remind the children of the sessions in *Dress Rehearsal* and the clothes they wore for each session.

Do this with a summary of God's big story as follows, asking the children to clarify details as you go along. Refer to the 'Big Cloth' as appropriate:

Everyone at the time of Noah was doing wrong things and so God wanted to start again, with Noah's family. God made a promise that he would never again destroy people as he had done by sending a flood. The sign of his promise was a rainbow. (Wet weather clothes)

God's people had to make themselves clean and ready to hear from God. And then God gave them rules to live by. They found it demanding to keep the rules or Ten Commandments as we know them. (Dirty clothes)

God's people continued to disobey God but through the prophet Jeremiah's visit to the potter, God promised to be faithful to his people. He made a new promise to them. (Protective clothing)

Jesus came to live in an ordinary community and he fed a large crowd of people, showing how God cared for people. (Sun hat)

Jesus also told stories which his enemies disliked – the story about the Samaritan who was looked down on but did the right thing in helping an injured man. (Bandage, plaster or sling.) Or the story of the son who ran away with much of his father's wealth but came back and was forgiven. (Old shoes and clothes)

Jesus' enemies succeeded in arresting Jesus which led to his unjust trial. He was put to death on a cross. But that was not the end, because two days later, he came alive again, in a new way. (Something red)

Throughout *Dress Rehearsal*, you have been looking at God's plan for the world and his promises to his people. God made time in the beginning and time is going to come to an end. We don't know when or how but the Bible does give us some clues. John, one of the early Christians, was sent to an island called Patmos (which was where some Roman prisoners were sent). There he had several visions about God's world, which included a vision about what would happen at the end of time. It is written down in the last book of the Bible, Revelation. God's people will go to live with God for ever, which we call heaven. But also, God is going to

make a new heaven and a new earth. It is going to be full of all things beautiful and will be the best ever. Nothing sad or wrong will be there. Right in the middle is where God will be.

At this point, show the DVD.

■ QUIZ
Alternatively, devise a quiz to help the children review God's big story.

②② Bible and me
5 minutes

You will need
• Bibles or *Into the Bible* (R101).

Either children can read Revelation 21:1–6; 22:1–5 for themselves, or ask them to listen to the verses read out loud and whenever they hear one of the key words below, they are to make a sign. Explain that Jerusalem was the city where Jesus was killed and is used here to mean all God's people.
• **New**: hold hands upright, palms out and shimmer them
• **Home**: cuddle oneself
• **Anything sad**: wipe an imaginary tear from the eye
• **Anything happy**: draw a smile in the air with a finger
• **Water/river**: a flowing movement

Arrange the children into small groups (each group with an adult helper).

This is a stunning passage using pictorial language. Ask the children to be still and think what is the best thing they have just heard.

Then ask them to share that best thing. Make sure the leaders have selected some of the key features of the new heaven and earth, such as no tears, pain, darkness, God being at home, plenty of fruit. Ask for quick feedback.

Comment that this is something amazing to look forward to. Explain that after you have talked with God, you are going to get ready for a banquet, as though it were a wedding, preparing the food, making something special to wear, arranging the table and so on.

2 3 **Conversation with God**
5 minutes

While we can look forward to what the new heaven will be like for all those who love God, we still live in a world where there is sadness and pain. Remind them that in the garden they heard about last session, the women's sadness was turned to joy when they knew that Jesus was alive again.

Give everyone a Post-it note and a pen. Ask them to write or draw something sad, difficult or painful that they want God to change. Give some topical suggestions for prayer. Invite everyone to bring their notes to a specific point, such as a cross, a rainbow, a Bible, candle or something that reminds them that God is faithful. Speak to God about these requests and thank him that he hears and responds!

2 4 **Learn and remember**
5 minutes

See how many of the Learn and remember verses the children can remember. Do this all together, so that those who have poor memories or haven't been to every session will not be excluded. You could include:

⊙ *God will make his home among his people.* ⊙
Revelation 21:3

Part three
Ready to go on stage

9 1 **Preparing for 'Showtime'/Construction**
15–30 minutes

There are many things you could do. Use as much gold and silver as you can, with other strong deep colours to emphasise the 'richness' of the event. This does not have to be expensive but needs to be carefully planned. For example, would a local haberdashers or craft shop give you some remnants of material? What do people in the congregation have to offer? Has anyone recently been involved in a wedding or a Christmas or family celebration and have some decorations left over?

■ **WEDDING CLOTHES**
Girls might love to make a hat or a fascinator (the feathery/flowery arrangements on a band or clip that some women wear to weddings), or a necklace or bracelet; boys might prefer to make a flower button hole or a glittery badge.

■ **WEDDING DECORATIONS**
Flower arrangements or table decorations, place mats or name tags; fairy lights, tinsel or candles; decorated plates and trays for the food. Children could create an invitation to give to the person who is coming to collect them if adults are only joining in at the end.

■ **BANQUET FOOD**
You don't need a lot but pile the plates high and give a choice. Everything could be tiny but tasty! Children can help lay the table and arrange the 'Big Cloth' for all to see. For example:
• If you played the fruit game, have as much fruit in small pieces as possible, including dried fruit – Revelation 22:2 would suggest at least 12 fruits would be appropriate
• Tiny sandwiches with fillings that children like
• Biscuits which the children have iced
• Small pieces of pizza
• A selection of crisps
• Tiny sausage rolls

Words from the prompter
The 'creative medium' used in this session is preparing food – at the end of the session the idea is for the group to celebrate a wedding feast together. The limits to what you can do are your imagination, the number of helpers you have, the time available and the amount of food that is appropriate. The children should create something beautiful which will remind them of the glorious ending of time and the final session of **Dress Rehearsal**. The overall atmosphere needs to be one of light and brightness along with abundance of colour and food (which does not mean vast amounts but a rich variety of food, drink and colour). You are creating something that resembles a wedding banquet.

8

8

Banquet time

Welcome parents and carers if they have just arrived. Explain what you have been doing this session. Comment that one of the parts of John's vision was that God was going to create a new heaven and a new earth and it was as though God's people were going to come to him, as a bride comes to meet her bridegroom. So you are going to have a wedding feast as the last action of *Dress Rehearsal*. After all, a wedding is a good reason to celebrate and in a wedding service, the bride and groom have promised to be together for the rest of their life (even though sometimes things go wrong). This banquet is to celebrate what will happen at the end of time, although we do not know much about it!

After everyone has eaten, show the 'Big Cloth' and remind people of some of the highlights of the club. You could mention the Learn and remember verses.

Thank everyone for joining in and make sure that details of the next club series/session or family/parenting/discipleship/seasonal events have been well advertised. Also, give clear details of Sunday services.

Make sure that if your community project is not yet complete, you make it clear what will happen to it!

Dress Rehearsal for a whole or half day

You may have picked up this book because you want to do something to sustain the work done at *Showstoppers!* Or it may be that you are looking for a special event for a Saturday morning or a full day over half-term. Or you may want to cover some of the material in *Dress Rehearsal* so that you can run the remaining sessions at a later date.

The *Dress Rehearsal* programme is very flexible and lends itself to adaptation. Needless to say, you should ensure that all your Safeguarding Children Procedures and health and safety provision is closely followed.

The following plan is for a reunion event or a whole day one-off event. The aims of this are:

- To welcome everyone and remind them of the good times that you all had during the holiday club. It is always amazing how pleased children are to meet up with their leaders and even some of the children who they may not have seen in the course of the school day.
- To remind them of what they discovered about Jesus in *Showstoppers!* but also to help every child make progress in their journey with God.
- To have a fun time, making sure to include any children who were not part of *Showstoppers!* All children from the holiday club could be encouraged to bring a friend with them.
- To have a chance to talk with parents and family members.
- To put on a really good 'Showtime'.
- To let everyone know about any forthcoming events in the church and the plans for the next holiday club.

Making a programme

Showstoppers! features

If you held a *Showstoppers!* holiday club, decide which elements of the club were the most successful and try to repeat them. This might include any popular songs, the Learn and remember verse, games, jokes and any characters who caused everyone to laugh. You will also want to show photos of the holiday club or have a rolling PowerPoint display.

Using the Dress Rehearsal material

Since dressing up is very much part of preparing for a show, and is a key part of *Dress Rehearsal*, you will need to decide how you are going to incorporate costumes and dressing up into the programme. You could have a fancy-dress parade specifying how the children should dress before they arrive. This would depend upon how many of the eight stories you want to develop.

Since this is longer than a club session, you have time to build some relationships in small groups. Put each child in a group with a leader(s) prepared to get to know them. These groups could be used for a Bible and Me time, for Conversation with God, for construction work, for food and for preparing for the final 'Showtime'. Of course, children may be given a choice about which activities they take part in, which will affect how the groups work.

You may want to give each child a gift from the event. This could be a copy of *The 10 Must Know*

Single day

Stories or *The Green Book of Must Know Stories*. It is suggested that the Bible stories you use come from the Green Book (which only contains five of the ten *Must Know* stories). Alternatively, you might want to give children a copy of *Into the Bible*. Contact Scripture Union Mail Order (0845 07 06 006) if you would like to arrange a bulk purchase of these books. You could also arrange for your local Christian bookshop to run a bookstall if many adults are going to be present.

Consider what sort of 'Showtime' you want to present. That will affect what stories and activities you will offer.

Younger children love dressing up. You could set up an area with plenty of dressing-up clothes and the scope for imaginary play. Base this around one of the stories you are presenting. For example, children might love to pretend they are in the ark, with various toy animals. They could pretend to be animals or Noah and his family. Or they could imagine the picnic scene on the hillside, beginning with getting the picnic ready in the kitchen. The imagination of the children will affect how much adult intervention is required. Alternatively, some younger children might like to play with Noah's ark Playmobil or Lego.

Suggested programmes

There are three programmes suitable for different times of the year. They will take children through six of the eight Bible stories in *Dress Rehearsal*.

Make sure that at the end of each day, everyone knows what is going to happen next – what the next *Dress Rehearsal* event will be! It could be that you are going to offer the sessions that have not been covered in this event in shorter midweek sessions. Or a holiday club could be the next item on your programme.

Programme one

This day covers Noah and the Ten Commandments. It would be suitable for autumn half-term, as the wet weather clothes link in very well to normal autumn wet weather!

01 Welcome

Including making or giving out badges. Make sure that parents/carers know when to come back for 'Showtime' at the end of the day. Introduce the Big Cloth here, so that children know what it is and that they can add to it. Give out wet weather clothes to any children who don't have them. If you are using *Dress Rehearsal* to follow up a *Showstoppers!* holiday club, then you could have the *Showstoppers!* song playing in the background.

02 Games/Audition time

Play some of the games from Session 1, page 18. Or, if you did *Showstoppers!*, you could do one of the Audition times which were popular.

03 Tell the story

Tell the story of Noah from *The 10 Must Know Stories* or page 50. See page 9 for guidance. Follow this up with 'Bible and me'.

04 Construction

Have fun making the potato men together. See page 20. Or produce something which can be added to the Big Cloth.

05 Preparation for Showtime

Work together to produce the sound story from page 50. This will form the 'Showtime' for the end of the day.

06 Lunch

You will need to decide before the session how you are going to cope with feeding the children. You could ask parents/carers to provide a packed lunch, or provide a simple lunch yourselves. You must make sure you comply with all the latest health and safety requirements. See the SU holiday club website for details.

07 Games

Do the washing activity from Session 2, page 21.

08 Tell the story

Tell the story of the Ten Commandments from *The 10 Must Know Stories* or page 52. See page 9 for guidance. Follow this up with the Learn and remember verse.

09 Conversation with God

Pray together using the activity from page 22.

010 Construction

Do the rag decorating activity from page 22, and stick the finished rags to the Big Cloth.

011 Showtime

When all the parents and carers have arrived, perform the Noah sound story which you rehearsed in 'Preparation for Showtime' earlier.

Single day

Programme two

This day covers the good Samaritan and the lost son. You could do this at Christmas time, but you may want to do a Christmas-themed day then, and use this day-long programme in the February half-term.

❷1 Welcome

Including making or giving out badges. Make sure that parents/carers know when to come back for 'Showtime' at the end of the day. Remind the children about the Big Cloth and show them the painted rags you did at the previous *Dress Rehearsal* day. Give out bandages to the children and help them put them on.

❷2 Games/Audition time

Play some of the races from Session 5, page 31. Or, if you did *Showstoppers!*, you could do one of the Audition times which the children enjoyed.

❷3 Bible and me

Set the scene for the story of the good Samaritan by using the 'Bible and me' activity from page 31. Follow this up with 'Tell the story', using the story from *The 10 Must Know Stories* or page 55.

❷4 Learn and remember verse

If possible, use the Learn and remember verse song from *Bitesize Bible Songs 1* (SU 978 184427 260 0), called 'Love the Lord'.

❷5 Construction

Spend some time making things for people who aren't well. Suggestions are on page 32.

❷6 Lunch

❷7 Games

Play the shoe-related parachute game from page 34.

❷8 Tell the story

Tell the story of the lost son, by reading the story from *The 10 Must Know Stories* or page 56. Follow this up with the 'Bible and me' section.

❷9 Conversation with God

Help the children pray together by using the activity on page 35.

❷10 Construction (extended)

Work together to make the film strips and box televisions from page 35. When you have finished, practise telling the story of the lost son, using these film strips, so that it can be part of 'Showtime'.

❷11 Showtime

When all the parents and carers have arrived, tell the story of the lost son using the film strips you have made.

Programme three

This day covers the stories of Jesus' trial and the end of time. It would be particularly suitable to be held during the Easter holidays.

1 Welcome

Including making or giving out badges. Make sure that parents/carers know when to come back for 'Showtime' at the end of the day. Remind the children about the Big Cloth. Give out strips of red ribbon or cloth for the children to tie onto themselves somewhere.

2 Games/Audition time

Play some of the races from Session 7, page 37. Or, if you did *Showstoppers!*, you could do one of the Audition times which the children enjoyed.

3 Tell the story

Use the 'Tell the story' activity from page 37 to help you tell the story of Jesus' trial. Follow this up with 'Bible and me'.

4 Conversation with God

Choose one of the prayer activities from pages 38–39 to help the children reflect on what they have just discovered.

5 Construction

Work together to produce the collages from page 39.

6 Lunch

7 Games

Play the Pass the parcel game from page 41, as this leads directly into the story.

8 Tell the story

Help the children discover more about Revelation 21 and 22 by using the 'Tell the story' activity on page 41. Follow this with 'Bible and me'.

9 Construction

Prepare the food for your wedding feast following the guidance on page 43.

10 Showtime (extended)

Celebrate together by eating the wedding feast together with the parents and carers.

An alternative would be to have a snack before the morning construction time and a late lunch that incorporates the wedding feast.

Resource pages

Telling the story

Each of the following stories has been reproduced with the permission of the author, Heather Butler.

Session one
God's promise to Noah

BOAT BUILDING ON DRY LAND

Narrator: Fighting, stealing, cheating, bullying – in every corner of the earth, it seemed like everything people thought and did was bad.

Group 1: One child says, 'I hate you!', another child joins in, 'I hate you!', a third joins in and so on until all children are shouting, 'I hate you!' together loudly. The shouting could then die down and a child could begin to quietly snivel, 'I'm bullied!'

Narrator: In the end God said:

God: I'm sorry I ever made them.

Narrator: Then he looked around to see if there was anyone left who might take him seriously. And he saw… Noah. An ordinary man who believed in God enough to listen and then do what he was told. He was also strong enough to cope with being laughed at. Noah was God's man.

God: I'm going to destroy everyone.

Group 2: all children take a sharp intake of breath and say, 'Oh, no!'

Narrator: Imagine Noah's face when he heard that. Then imagine his face when he heard the next bit.

God: Get some strong wood and build a boat. You're going to build it on dry land, not water. Put rooms in it and give it a roof to keep out the rain. Make it 133 m long.

Narrator: Longer than a football pitch.

Group 2: That's very long!

God: 22 m wide.

Narrator: That's twice the distance from the penalty spot to the goal-line.

Group 2: That's very wide!

God: And 13 m high.

Narrator: Higher than a pile of three double-decker buses.

Group 2: That's very high!

God: Make it three floors high with just one door on the side. I promise that all your family – you, your wife, your three sons and their wives – will be kept safe in the boat.

When you go into the boat take with you a male and female of every kind of animal, bird and reptile that there is. And food to feed them all.

Narrator: Noah was going to be a master builder, a ship's captain and a chief zookeeper. He was going to be very busy.

Noah needed so much wood that he had to ship in logs from forests far away. (Well not "ship" exactly since this was all on dry land.) He mixed bucket-loads of tar to daub on the outside walls, the roof and then the insides as well.

Group 3: all children make sounds of a building site, eg rattling the inside of a bucket, banging sticks of wood together, banging a hammer on wood – ask the group for suggestions.

Narrator: While he was doing this, people came on day trips to see what was happening. They fell about laughing. What madman would build a boat in the middle of dry land? And why build it so long and wide and tall? Then they went home again.

All groups: everyone laughs and jeers loudly.

Narrator: At last the boat was finished. It towered above the trees and fields around it. The day trippers clapped and cheered.

Group 1: But how will you get it to water?

Group 2: It's too heavy to drag anywhere and too wide for our river.

All groups: everyone laughs and jeers loudly.

Narrator: Noah knew the answer to their question. God had told him that in seven days' time it would begin to rain. It wouldn't stop for 40 days and 40 nights. The earth would be flooded. That meant Noah had just seven days to collect all the animals. That's not very long.

All groups: everyone makes animal noises in turn. At the end, all the sounds could be made at the same time in a noisy outburst!

Narrator: But a week later, Noah, his wife, his three sons and their wives stood by their huge boat now stuffed with noisy, smelly, restless creatures. Was it really going to rain? They still didn't know as they climbed inside. The door banged shut behind them. It was God who had shut the door.

All groups: everyone shouts, "BANG!" and intentionally jumps.

Narrator: That day the sky opened its windows and the rivers and underground streams burst. The day trippers rushed home, afraid their homes would be washed away. On and on the water gushed until the boat started to float. Before long all the trees and the tracks, the hills and homes disappeared – everything except one tar-covered boat bobbing on the surface of the water.

Group 1: all the children make the sound of raindrops, starting with a slow pitter-patter, then getting louder and faster. Or water could be poured from one container to another. The sound effects should continue until the rain stops.

Narrator: The pitter-patter on the roof went on and on and on. The water covering the land was unimaginably deep. Did any of the animals inside the boat have babies?

Group 3: We don't know!

Narrator: Did they get sea-sick?

Group 3: We don't know!

Narrator: Did Noah and his wife argue?

Group 3: We don't know!

Narrator: We'll never know, but we do know that God did not forget them. After 40 days the rain stopped.

The silence outside seemed strange after the noisy pitter-patter. Slowly, very slowly, the water levels began to drop. But it took 150 days before Noah heard a scraping sound. The bottom of the boat had struck the rocks on top of the Ararat Mountains.

Narrator: But Noah waited 40 more days. Then he carried a raven to the top floor. The raven got very excited when it saw open skies through the gap between the wall and the roof. It unfurled its wings, thought of doing a loop-the-loop, changed its mind and circled high. No way was it going back inside! It kept flying round and round and round for days and days searching for land.

Group 2: all children make suitable sounds for the raven and then the dove.

Narrator: A while later Noah carried a dove to the top floor. It cooed gently as it squeezed through the gap. Doing wing stretches and press-ups in cramped conditions was no joke. It flew off but before long it came back. It couldn't find any branches to land. So Noah had to wait another seven days before he released the dove again. This time it flew back with a single green olive leaf in its beak. Noah grinned. Leaves meant trees. Trees meant plants. Plants meant food. Food meant getting off this boat!

Yet still Noah waited one more week. He sent out the dove and this time it didn't return. Noah jumped up and down in excitement.

All groups: Everyone makes a jumping sound.

Narrator: Then he smashed a hole in the roof of the boat.

Group 1: everyone makes a breaking wood sound.

Narrator: Then he popped his head up. He breathed in huge gulps of fresh air, gasping at the sunlight, the land and the mountains. He was alive. His family was safe.

All groups: everyone cheers! You could repeat the animal sounds in order as they too cheer!

Narrator: God told Noah to leave the boat. He couldn't get out fast enough. He felt wobbly to be walking on dry land and stretching his arms wide without hitting anything. The very first thing Noah did was to thank God. And God said:

God: I will never again punish the earth like this. As long as the earth remains people will plant seeds and harvest them. Winter and summer, day and night will come and go. Whenever you see a rainbow, just remember this promise.

All groups: everyone gasps with wonder and then cheers!

Narrator: Noah looked up. High above him a glorious rainbow arched its back and reached down to the earth – red, orange, yellow, green, blue, indigo, violet. Wow!

Resources

Session two
The Ten Commandments

THE BIG CLEAN UP

'We'll set up camp right here!'

It was the voice of Moses, the old man who had led the people in their dramatic escape from Egypt. That was two months ago. Since then they had been moving slowly, setting up a camp, moving on again, setting up camp, moving on and setting up camp.

These people were all from one large family, thousands and thousands of them who all shared the same great, great, great, great (and a few more) grandfather. His name was Israel. They had been slaves in Egypt for almost more years than anyone could remember. Their slave masters had beaten them. Now, it was fantastic to have escaped, but it was scary too. Would life be better? Where were they going? Did Moses really know what he was doing? After all, he was an old man and had grown up as an Egyptian prince. He had never really lived with these people or known what it was like to be a slave. But he had said, 'We'll set up camp right here!' So that was what they were doing.

They dropped their bundles and sighed with tiredness. The ground was rough and hard, as you would expect at the bottom of a mountain. But there was a stream close by and there was shelter from the wind. Before long, tents were being put up and places found for the animals to graze. Fires were lit, water was boiling and food was being prepared. This was their life in the desert. But it was better than in Egypt.

Within days of arriving, Moses climbed up the mountain behind the campsite. He met God there. It was all very mysterious but he looked fairly cheerful when he reappeared.

'God has told me he will keep us safe if we do what he says. We'll be known as the people of God!' He had also said he was going to speak with Moses and everyone would hear the conversation.

Wow! Actually speak with God! Moses gave some very clear instructions. They had three days to get themselves ready. Everyone, absolutely everyone, had to wash themselves all over and put on clean clothes. They had to be clean because they were meeting with God, who was pure.

Getting ready to meet God was hard work. Their clothes were made out of such heavy cloth that it took ages for them to dry, even in the hot sun.

But three days later everyone, absolutely everyone, had clean bodies and clean clothes. They waited, in the campsite. Children hopped from one foot to another. Adults whispered anxiously. In the middle of the crowd, a child pointed at the mountain. Those around followed her finger. Everyone could see. There was no missing it now. The top of the mountain was being covered in a thick, swirling cloud of smoke. No one had ever seen anything like this before. Moses beckoned and led the people towards the foot of the mountain. God's orders were that no one was to step onto the mountain itself.

As they stood there with Moses in front, the loudest, most terrifying blast erupted from inside the mountain. Later they described it as sounding like a trumpet vibrating and exploding in each person's ear. Smoke belched upwards and sideways and out in all directions. Then the earth began to shake and rattle; louder and louder still. The smoke was now hovering just above peoples' heads, hot and fiery. In the middle of this they heard a voice calling Moses to come back up the mountain.

For an old man Moses was very strong. The people watched him get smaller and smaller until he disappeared into the smoke. Would he ever come back?

Hours passed and the people waited. Lunchtime came and went. No one ate anything. The afternoon sun began to sink in the sky. And still they waited. At last, they saw a figure moving down the mountain, out of the smoke. It was Moses. In silence they watched him stride towards them.

Somehow, at the top of the mountain, surrounded by the smoke and rumbles, God had spoken to Moses and given him instructions for his people. These instructions were how God, who was pure, wanted his people to behave. So in front of the people, still in their clean clothes (with smoke smuts all over them) Moses told the people what God had said.

One. I am the Lord your God. I brought you out of Egypt where you were slaves. Don't worship any other god, except me.

(In other words, someone explained to his children, 'Remember who God is, so don't be tempted to put your trust in anything or anyone else – not that you're likely to after today.')

Two. Do not make idols.

(In other words, someone else whispered, 'Don't draw pictures or make statues of God and worship them.')

Three. Do not misuse my name.

('That includes breaking promises after swearing something is true or using God's name when you haven't thought about it. God's name is special.')

Four. Remember I made the world in six days then rested. You must rest every seventh day.

('The rule is six days on, one day off.')

Five. Respect your father and your mother.

('Listen to that one, son. Don't forget it. Families are very important.')

Six. Do not murder.

('Life is a gift from God.')

Seven. Be faithful in marriage.

('Families again.')

Eight. Do not steal.

('Don't take anything that isn't yours.')

Nine. Do not tell lies.

('Be completely honest.')

Ten. Do not look at anything that belongs to someone else and want it for yourself.

('Jealousy is bad for you.')

This was serious stuff. The people had made themselves clean for this day. God now wanted them to go on living clean lives. So the people of God (for that was what they were) walked back to the campsite. No photographs, no videos, no films, no sound tracks, but the memory of this day would be fixed in their minds for ever.

Session four
Feeding over 5,000

AND THE REST...

Nat and his little brother had chased lizards most of the way up the hill. Their mother kept getting cross with them, telling them to stick to the path. They had come all this way to listen to Jesus, the visiting storyteller, not to chase lizards. Mum had said he was worth listening to. Crowds of other people had had the same idea.

When they reached the grass on the hillside where Jesus was telling his stories, one of Jesus' friends showed them where to sit. They pushed through the crowd and ended up just three rows from the front. It gave them a good view and meant they could hear and see everything. Nat was soon caught up in the stories and cheered with everyone else when Jesus made sick people well again.

As usual, his tummy started rumbling and before long he was asking Mum for something to eat. He knew there were lentils and olives and other bits of food in her basket. Eating these with fingers was messy but mess doesn't matter when you're eating outside.

Nat still felt hungry. 'Save the rest for later,' his mum said and pulled the basket away.

It was 'the rest' Nat thought about when, much later in the day, he overheard a conversation between two of Jesus' friends, or 'disciples' as Mum called them.

'We'll have to tell Jesus to send the people away so they can go to the villages round here and find food and somewhere to stay.'

'This is such a lonely place. Everyone will be so hungry.'

Nat frowned. All day Jesus had been making people better. People who couldn't walk were carried up the hill on stretchers. They had run back down the path. Blind people shuffled over towards Jesus helped by friends and family – and then suddenly they could see. Deaf people no longer needed someone to shout at them. Nat didn't quite understand. Surely, making food would be a piece of cake. It would just be like making people better. Why were the disciples saying everyone should go home?

Nat ferreted around in his mother's basket. 'The rest' he was thinking about were some barley loaves and fish. They were a bit squashed. He took them out and tugged at the coat of the disciple standing near to him.

'I've got some small, barley bread loaves and some fish here.'

'How many?'

'One, two, three, four, five,' Nat counted.

'And how many fish?'

'One, two.'

The disciple wrinkled his nose, thought a bit, then grinned.

'Come with me,' he said.

Nat followed until they stood in front of Jesus. He held out the squashed barley loaves (his brother had sat on them) and the two small fish (they were flat already).

'Here are five loaves and two fish,' the disciple spoke into Jesus' ear.

Jesus looked at Nat and then at the bread and fish. They didn't look much at all, but Jesus nodded and smiled.

'Get everyone to sit down in groups of about 50,' he said.

Then Jesus held up two of the loaves, one in each hand, looked up to heaven and thanked God for the food. Slowly he began breaking up all five loaves into small pieces. He did the same with the fish. Nat saw what Jesus was doing and gasped. The more Jesus broke up the bread and fish, the more there was. And before long everyone was cheering and holding out their hands as the disciples were giving out the food. Nat was one of the first to get some.

He saved a bit for his brother who had fallen asleep. Mum was going to have to carry him home. That meant Nat would have to carry his mum's basket.

Jesus' friends had begun to pick up the crumbs of food still lying on the ground. In the end they filled twelve huge baskets with the bread and fish pieces. There had been more then enough for everyone to eat. Nat picked up his basket. It was a long walk home!

Session five
The Good Samaritan

Narrator: Larry is a lizard. He hangs around waiting for things to happen. Today he is at his favourite place - a big, grey rock next to the road. From there he watches life.

Larry: Love this place - flat rock to myself, cool cracks to drop into if it gets too hot, people passing. What else could a lizard ask for? To my left is Jerusalem (twenty three hours of scurrying). The other way is Jericho (seventeen hours). People travel from Jerusalem to Jericho and back all the time. I see them all.

And here come the first people of the day. Two men, churning up a cloud of dust behind them, running towards me. Now they've stopped, panting, by my rock. I drop into a crack, then peep out at them. They might be lizard hunters. They're sweating. One has an eye patch. The other's arm is decorated with a deep scar. Something tells me they're bad news.

Eye Patch sees me and turns away. So they are not lizard hunters. But why are they lurking behind my rock? They've stopped whispering. Deep Scar has taken a knife out of his pocket. Eye Patch is clutching a stick. I do not like these two. A man is coming towards us humming a little song. Is he happy or is he nervous?

Eye Patch and Deep Scar have jumped out from behind the rock. They have beaten Humming Man. Now he is lying on the ground in a pool of blood. Why did they kick him so hard? They've stolen his money and are running away. Humming Man is not humming any more. He is dragging himself towards my rock.

Humming Man has pulled his coat over his face. He needs water. It is very hot. The ground is dusty. But, here comes someone who will help, a man walking briskly towards Jerusalem. His fancy clothes are what a priest wears. He must work in the temple. Surely he will be kind. Looks like Humming Man has heard him. He's raises his hand. Fancy Dress Man looks across. But he does not stop! He is in a hurry. He walks by very fast, on the other side of the road. I stick my neck out. When I am angry it quivers and goes red. It is red now. Very red. Fancy Dress Man has disappeared down the road. Humming Man's head has flopped back into the dust.

Humming Man's lips are parched. The blood on his face has turned a brownish colour. But here comes someone who might help - one of Fancy Dress Man's friends. He has a different coloured coat but I know he works in the Temple too. Humming Man has heard him. He lifts his head a little and moans. But Temple Man ignores him and walks by quickly, on the other side. I stick out my neck again. It is has gone even redder than very red.

Humming Man is getting worse. He is not moving any more. I am very worried.

This road has not been very busy today. But here comes what may be Humming Man's last chance - a man on a slowly moving donkey. This man looks like he comes from the region called Samaria. That makes him a Samaritan. Samaritans are hated by people from round here. Humming Man, are you going to be saved by someone you hate? Samaritan has stopped and is sliding off his donkey's back. His knees creak as he kneels beside Humming Man. Samaritan goes back to his donkey. He pulls a piece of cloth out of his bag and rips it up to make a bandage. He's got wine and oil, too.

Samaritan helps Humming Man sit up. He pours oil on his cuts and gives him a drink. Now he is helping him onto the back of his donkey. I had better hang onto the donkey's tail if I am going to see what happens next.

We've stopped at a guest house. It'll be cool inside. Samaritan lifts Humming Man off the donkey. He calls for someone to help carry Humming Man inside. There's a chink of money. Samaritan is paying for Humming Man to stay.

Samaritan: If you need more money, I will pay you next time I am passing by.

Larry: What a hero! Samaritan doesn't even know this man he has helped. He ought to be called 'A Good Samaritan'!

Resources

Session six
The tale of two sons

Jesus sat down. His eyes swept slowly over the crowd who were waiting for another story. Children squeezed to the front, enjoying a family outing. Adults glanced at the temple leaders who were hovering like vultures at the edge of the crowd. They were unhappy with what Jesus said and how he treated everyone in the same way. Why, they asked themselves, did Jesus bother with ordinary people like these? Most of them were no-hopers!

Jesus was ready. The crowd was quiet. The storyteller could begin.

"There was a man with two sons. The younger son was not happy. (The older son was not happy either but more of that later.)

'Give me my share of everything you own,' the younger son said to his father one day. Just like that. He knew that when his dad died, everything would be shared between him and his brother. But he wanted the money now. To spend.

To his delight and surprise, his father did as he asked, dividing everything into two equal parts. The older son watched. He saw the smile on his brother's face grow as the pile of money, sheep, goats, bits of furniture, cooking pots, tools, **clothes and shoes**, and anything else got bigger and bigger and bigger. The older son was not happy. The younger son was.

Smugly, the younger son packed his bags.

'Ta-ra!' he called over his shoulder. Money clinked in his pocket, sheep bleated behind him and cartwheels rattled over the bumpy track. He was taking what was his. He planned to go to a foreign country where no one knew him. There would be no big brother keeping an eye on him and no father watching what he did. His father could be dead for all he cared.

Before long he had a house in his new country. He could do what he liked with his money. And he did – parties, shopping, more parties, more shopping, a bigger house, new clothes, **dazzling shoes**, a few more parties. His new friends helped him. His new friends were good at helping him – until there was no money left. Then they disappeared. A famine had come to that country, so to add to his troubles there was little food to eat. No money, no food, no friends, no job, no family, no hope – no wonder he was desperate.

At that time, pigs were cared for by no-hopers. There was no worse job. The younger son was so desperate that he went to the local pig farmer and offered to look after the pigs. His clothes were in rags; **his shoes were full of holes**. It got so bad that he even ate the swill of the pigs he was looking after.

One day he said to himself, 'My father's workers have plenty to eat back home and here I am, starving to death! I will go to my father and say to him, "Dad, I have wronged God in heaven and wronged you. I've wasted all your money and treated you dreadfully. I am no longer good enough to be called your son. Can I have a job on the farm because at least your workers have enough to eat?"'

So the younger son set off for home – no money clinking in his pockets, no sheep bleating, no cartwheels rattling over the bumpy track and **no shoes on his feet**. He was a broken man with just the hope that his father would allow him to work for him.

What the younger son did not know was that at least once a day since he had left home, his father had walked to the edge of the village and stared up the track his son had taken when he left. Every day he hoped his son would come home. And on this particular day he had gone to the edge of the village around lunchtime. He looked up the track and… there was his son, kicking up stones, head bowed, trudging along the road.

The father recognised him immediately. Without a second thought, he hitched up his long coat and charged towards his son. He flung his arms out wide in welcome.

'My son! You've come home!' he yelled, so loud that every one in the village must have heard.

But his son did not run into his dad's arms. He did not smile. He didn't even look pleased. Instead he dropped at his father's feet and sobbed.

'I have wronged you and God…' How many times had he practised saying this? 'I'm not good enough to be called your son. Can I just be a worker on your farm?'

The father heard the sadness in his voice. It didn't matter to him that his younger son smelt of pigs and sweat, or that he had as good as wished his father dead. He pulled his son to his feet and looked deep into his son's eyes. Then he hugged him as he had never hugged him before.

His son was forgiven and to prove it he put a ring on his son's finger. This was a sign of being part of the family. Then he found him some new clothes and some **brand new shoes**.

'This son of mine was as good as dead,' he kept telling everyone, 'but he's come back to life. It's time for a party!'

Before long, meat sizzled over the fire, the table was spread with the best food and there was music, laughter and dancing. What a party!

But then… the older son came home, striding out in his **working shoes**, as he did every day after working hard in the fields. He hadn't seen his father race along the track. But as he got closer, he smelt meat cooking.

'What's going on?' he asked one of the servants.

'Your brother's come home.'

'Why's he come home? And why throw a party for him?'

The servant swallowed hard. This older son was not happy.

Just then his father joined them. 'Come on, you're missing the party,' he said.

'No way am I going to party!' the older son spat in rage. 'For years I've worked for you. I've done everything you asked me to do. But you've never given a party for my friends. But as soon as this pathetic, selfish brother of mine comes home, that's just what you do! It's not fair!'

The father sighed. 'Everything I have is yours. You are always with me. Come on. Your brother's return is worth a celebration!'"

Jesus paused. A lizard scurried across the ground. The older brothers at the edge of the crowd muttered to themselves. Why did Jesus tell stories about no-hopers that had happy endings?

This story has been slightly amended (with the author's permission) to tie in with the shoe theme.

Playdough recipes

'Cooked' playdough

You will need

- 2 cups plain flour
- 2 tablespoons cream of tartar
- 1½ cups water
- ½ cup of salt
- 1 tablespoon oil
- A few drops of food colouring

Method

Mix together flour and cream of tartar. Boil water, salt, oil and food colouring in a saucepan. Stir liquid into the flour, allow to cool, then knead until smooth. Cool further before letting children use it.

If you wrap this dough in a couple of polythene bags it will keep for some time in a fridge. Obviously small children should be discouraged from eating this, though the high salt content and the cream of tartar usually ensure they only taste it once!

Uncooked playdough

(makes enough for 8-10 children)

You will need

- 4 cups plain flour
- 2 cups water
- 2 cups salt
- 2 tablespoons cooking oil
- Food colouring

Method

Add salt to flour, and gradually add the water and oil, stirring constantly. When everything is well mixed, sprinkle work top with flour and knead dough. (This can be done in an electric mixer with a dough hook attachment.)

This dough will not last as long as the cooked variety but is fine in an emergency or if you have no cooking facilities.

For more play dough recipes, see *Ultimate Craft* (SU 978 184427 364 5).

Eagle

Resources

Ultimate series

Do you work with children or young people? Need that extra bit of inspiration to help your group explore the Bible? Want that extra idea to complete your session?

Then the **Ultimate** series is for you!

Each **Ultimate** book is packed full of ideas that have been used successfully by others and are more than likely to work for you!

All at £9.99

Ultimate Craft 978 1 84427 364 5

Ultimate Creative Prayer 978 1 84427 367 6

Ultimate Games 978 1 84427365 2

Ultimate Quizzes 978 1 84427 366 9

Ultimate Visual Aids CD ROM 978 1 84427 355 3

Order from SU Mail Order
Phone 0845 07 06 006
Fax 01908 856 020
Online www.scriptureunion.org.uk/shop

Resources to use alongside
DRESS REHEARSAL

FOR LEADERS

Must Know Stories

The *Must Know Stories* are a way
of restoring understanding of the
importance of ten key stories in the
Bible – ten stories that have been voted
on as essential to our culture and which
teachers and parents feel must not be
lost to the next generation.

Robert Harrison
978 1 84427 320 1
£7.99

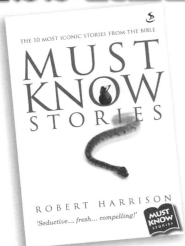

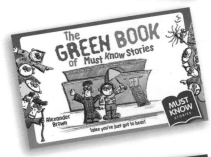

FOR CHILDREN

For 5 to 8s:
The Red Book of
Must Know Stories

Five of the *Must Know Stories* voted as those
most needing to be passed onto the next
generation. Young readers will really enjoy
engaging with five of these stories written and
wonderfully illustrated by Alexander Brown.
The five stories are: Adam and Eve, David and
Goliath, Daniel in the lions' den, the birth of
Jesus, Jesus comes back to life.

Alexander Brown
978 1 84427 325 6
£3.99

Also available:
The Green Book of
Must Know Stories

Five of the ten *Must Know Stories,* voted as those
Bible stories most needing to be passed onto the
next generation. Young readers will really enjoy
the storytelling and wonderful illustrations of
Alexander Brown. The five in this book are:
Noah's ark, Ten commandments, feeding over
5000, the good Samaritan, the prodigal son.

Alexander Brown
978 1 84427 324 9
£3.99

For 8 to 11s
The 10 Must Know Stories

This collection of ten stories is a refreshing
read. Children who are competent readers
will encounter the ten Bible stories voted
as the ones that most need to be passed
onto the next generation.

Heather Butler
978 1 84427 326 3
£3.99

Resources

Other resources from Scripture Union to help you with midweek clubs

Clubs website

We have recently updated our website to give you even more help in running your midweek club.

At **www.scriptureunion.org.uk/Clubs** you can download essential information about running a club such as child protection, health and safety issues and training your team. You can find out about all our current midweek club programmes and download the extra resources to the club of your choice as well as ordering any of the resources online.

Become part of the forum at the clubs website to share ideas of what has worked for you or for inspiration or encouragement from others.

Top Tips

Top Tips are booklets written by expert practitioners designed for all those working with children and young people. They're big on practical advice, but small enough to digest over a cup of coffee. We have a large selection of titles ranging from handling difficult behaviour to explaining the cross. For more details go to **www.scriptureunion.org.uk**

Lifepath

Lifepath is a Scripture Union project to help Christians in local communities organise an event to which they can invite local schools. It aims to give Junior school pupils the opportunity to explore the Christian faith through the lifepath of a well known historic Christian with a link to the location and to use this as a springboard to encourage them to reflect on their own lifepath.

As an event, *Lifepath*
- happens in term time during the school day with teachers present
- can work in indoor or outdoor venues
- can take a story from any century
- can last for as many days as there are schools wanting to attend
- can happen at any point in the school year.

For more details go to:
www.scriptureunion.org.uk/lifepath
or telephone **01908 856120**
or email **lifepath@scriptureunion.org.uk**

X:site

X:site is a town, area or city-wide children's event for anyone who is 7 to 11 years old. Events happen every two months and everyone that goes has lots of fun whilst learning more about God. They have such a great time that they invite their friends to come too. Each event combines silly games, live music with a great band, videos, creative prayer, craft, drama, Bible stories and lots more!

Check out the website **www.xsiteuk.org** for more details.

Training events

Scripture Union workers and volunteers run a variety of training courses throughout the year on topics such as how to be a church for all ages, or skills to grow faith in young people. For more details go to **www.scriptureunion.org.uk/News/Events**

eye level clubs...

- are for boys and girls aged 5 to 11.

- are for children who are not yet part of a church (as well as those who are).

- don't assume that children know much about Jesus or have had any experience of church.

- recognise that all children are open to God and the wonder of his world, and that all children can have valid spiritual experiences, regardless of church background.

- aim to give children one of the best hours in their week.

- provide opportunities for appropriate and respectful relationships between children and adults, working in small groups.

- plan to introduce children to the Bible in ways that allow for imagination, exploration and learning difficulties.

- are led by those who long to see children become lifelong followers of Jesus Christ.

- are led by those who will put themselves at a child's level, so that together they can catch sight of Jesus.